THAT I M MESSIAH

כדי שאהרויח את המשיח

a Messianic Jewish Devotional

KEVIN GEOFFREY

A ministry of Perfect Word Ministries

www.perfectword.org
1-888-321-PWMI

All Scripture quotations are from the Messianic Jewish Literal Translation of the New Covenant Scriptures (MJLT NCS).

ISBN #: 978-0-9837263-5-7

Cover art by Esther Geoffrey
Photo by Marc-Olivier Jodoin on Unsplash

Printed in the United States of America

For Esther, Isaac, Josiah, Hosea & Asher

You are my heart.

CONTENTS

A WORD FROM KEVIN

FOR TWENTY-TWO YEARS—the present age of my eldest son —Messianic devotionals have been a part of my life and ministry. I am grateful beyond words that so many have found them not only inspiring but challenging, and consider them worthy to be made a part of their daily time with God.

Much has happened in the thirteen years since Perfect Word last published a devotional book, and I am delighted that the time has finally come for a fresh volume. I am especially pleased with this particular collection because not only did I write them as an older and (hopefully) wiser man, but they were born out of my love for the Scriptures which is engraved on every page, chapter, verse, word, and letter of Perfect Word's recent Bible translation—upon which these devotionals are based.

After we published the *Messianic Jewish Literal Translation of the New Covenant Scriptures (MJLT NCS)* in 2018, I spent the following year working six mornings a week on brand new devotionals derived from the text of this incredible version of the Scriptures. While some of this work spilled over into the following year, that one year of devotional writing is essentially what is represented in this book. The passages of Scripture used in my three previous devotional books— *Messianic Daily Devotional, Messianic Mo'adiym Devotional* and *Messianic Torah Devotional*—were based on my cursory modernization of Young's Literal Translation, but now having majorly revised Young's as the framework of the MJLT, the resulting quality of the translation has only enhanced the clarity of the devotionals.

Since the MJLT is a translation of only the "New Testament," the 120 devotionals of *That I May Gain Messiah* are exclusively from that portion of the Scriptures. However, like the MJLT NCS itself, this should in no way be taken as a slight to the rest of Scripture, which is copiously represented in my other devotional books. In addition, by focusing only on this section of the Bible, *That I May Gain Messiah* is able to walk the reader through the New Covenant Scriptures in the order in which the books appear in the MJLT, which is primarily chronological. In this way, the reader is sure to come away with a unique experience not afforded by the traditional order of books of the New Testament.

The title of *That I May Gain Messiah* comes from Philippians 3:8 in which Paul writes, "I count all things to be loss... so that I may gain Messiah." It is as fundamental a biblical theme as there ever was, being espoused also by the Master Yeshua in מַתִּתְיָהוּ Matit'yahu 16:25 when He teaches us, "For whoever wants to save his life will lose it, and whoever loses his life for My sake will find it." Though it has been largely lost among believers today, this principal goal of salvation, discipleship and service to God remains the central point of the New Covenant Scriptures and therefore the underlying message of this compilation of devotionals.

As I've written previously concerning the daily discipline of devotion,

> each of us is in a different stage of life, with varying responsibilities, pressures, and other demands on our time and energy. As disciples of Messiah, however, we cannot afford to allow *life* to dictate how we *live*. The only way we can ever hope to gain control over our lives is to yield ourselves completely to God. Though we may prefer it to

be otherwise, such surrender is not a one-time event—it is ongoing, and requires a daily commitment. Undying devotion to God is key to living an effective, useful, *and happy* life for Messiah.

To the generous and faithful friends and partners of Perfect Word and MJMI, our board members, and especially my family, thank you for all your love, prayers and support—for helping me continue to teach and proclaim the truth of God's word.

And to you, the reader, my prayer is that as you read these pages, your heart, mind and spirit will be receptive to the self-examination, convicted by the exhortation, responsive to the edification, and ready and open to change. I pray that whatever God reveals to you about His word or about yourself, you will be willing to embrace it and become the effective disciple of Messiah that He has remade you to be.

I hope *That I May Gain Messiah* will be a blessing to you, building you up in the faith, action and boldness of the Master Yeshua. Let us each commit ourselves to remaining apart from the world and the flesh, count all things as loss for the sake of the Holy One, and gain the only thing we should ever truly long to have in this life and the next.

In the service of our Master the Messiah Yeshua,

Kevin Geoffrey
August 9, 2021

THAT I MAY GAIN
MESSIAH

כדי שאהרויח את המשיח

HAPPY ARE THOSE

> "Happy *are* those *who are* mourning—because they
> will be comforted." –מַתִּתְיָהוּ MATIT'YAHU 5:4

In times of great duress and uncertainty, it is often little
comfort to be told that everything will be all right. Positive
affirmations may be kind, but they only go so far, as they
cannot predict the future any more than they can guarantee
its outcome. But still, we offer reassurance to one another
(and ourselves) in the attempt to bring peace to an otherwise
utterly unpeaceful circumstance, hoping that our words will
assuage fears and create an alternate reality in our minds that
we can hold onto.

Yet the notion of advocating happiness for unhappy situations
seems, at first blush, totally tone deaf. If my situation should
naturally and reasonably cause unhappiness, why try telling
me that I am actually happy—or, at least, that I ought to
be? It seems silly at best, and cruel at worst—illogical, self-
contradictory, ridiculous and stupid. Reality is real, and we
cannot shut our eyes to avoid or ignore it in the empty hope
that when we open our eyes again, things will no longer be
exactly as they actually are. Happy situations cause happiness;
unhappy ones do not. That is reality.

But what if you knew that your bad situation was temporary,
and, more than that, that it had a purpose? And what if you
knew that even in the middle of distress, help was on its way?
That might be enough to make you happy. And what if the
feeling of happiness—or what you presently understand to be
how happiness feels—is not what happiness is at all? What
if you could experience true happiness by rising above your

circumstances, not forgetting or ignoring them, but seeing them from the perspective of someone who actually has the power to the alter the outcome—someone who will ultimately completely take care of you, no matter how things turn out? That might be enough to make you happy, too.

In Yeshua, our reality is not altered, but neither is it limited only to that which we can immediately see. Though we may be poor in ruach, we are rich in our inheritance in Heaven. Though we may be mourning in the material world, we will be comforted by God forever. True happiness in every circumstance comes from the pursuit of righteousness, as well as the future fullness which that righteousness brings. A bad situation does not bring happiness, but our response to it can. Happiness is knowing hope when we would otherwise be hopeless; happiness is having purpose when we would otherwise be purposeless. In Yeshua, we are given all heavenly hope and every perfect purpose...

...so what's not to be happy about?

PRAYER

Father, I am distressed and uncertain—my situation is bad and seems to be only getting worse. I feel hopeless because I feel helpless—how, then, can I feel happy? So I am calling out to You, ADONAI, for salvation from my circumstances. But if I should remain where I am, just show me Your face, and I will remember my reward. In You, Yeshua, I find all righteousness, purpose, peace and hope. You, my Master, are all I need in order to see the fullness of my reality, and to be, once and for all, truly happy.

THEY WHO ARE WHOLE

> "They who are whole have no need of a physician; rather, they who are ill." –מַתִּתְיָהוּ MATIT'YAHU 9:12

We rush to the hospital in times of emergency; we seek treatment for our medical conditions, both chronic and acute. We pop pharmaceuticals and natural supplements like they're candy; we exercise and we eat healthy foods with the hope of *avoiding* supplements, pharmaceuticals, doctors and hospitals. Physical illness or debility is a fact of life, and the older we get, the more effort it takes to counter the inevitable. But despite the fact that no one ever wants to be physically infirmed, eventually, we will all reach our expiration dates.

Our need for doctors, then, is driven by our desire to survive—to live in health. While some of us will run to urgent care the second we have a sneeze, and some of us will avoid doctors and hospitals like the plague, we each have a threshold—or a loved one—that leaves us no choice. There eventually comes a point when we are ready to admit we are ill—so ill, in fact, that we can no longer adequately treat ourselves—and we will finally seek out a physician. Indeed, who would ever volunteer to see a doctor while he is well?

And that is the Master's simple point: "They who are whole have no need of a physician; rather, they who are ill." But what of the patient who does not recognize his own illness—who has not a physical malady, but a spiritual one? What doctor is licensed to treat him? This is why the Master responded the way He did when confronted for His association with "sinners": because sinners are—spiritually speaking—sick. Mankind has a universal birth defect that physical treatment cannot overcome, for there is no medication to cure unrighteousness.

The Master Yeshua, our Great Physician, "did not come to call righteous men, but sinners"—and "there is none righteous, not even one" (Romans 3:10). The healthcare we receive from Yeshua is the only kind that will ever be truly universal and free—yet it will cost us our pride, our acknowledgment that we are sick, and our strength and will for the rest our lives. More than anything else, every man, woman and child—young and old, healthy and ill—needs the remedy for our shared disease that only the Master Yeshua can prescribe. Will you entrust every part of your life to the hands of the Great Physician, or will you wait to pay Him a visit until it is too late?

PRAYER

Master Yeshua—matchless and blameless one—please save me from my sin. Cleanse me, O God, and set me free from the affliction and disease that has been born into my flesh. I trust Your word, ADONAI, in both sickness and in health; teach me to rely only on Your perfect course of treatment. Help me, Master, to stop avoiding coming to see You, but to admit the severity of my disease, to find You, and to be healed.

THE ANXIETY OF THE AGE

> "And that *seed* sown toward the thorns: this is he who is hearing the word, yet the anxiety of the age and the deceitfulness of the wealth choke the word, and it becomes unfruitful."
>
> –מַתִּתְיָהוּ MATIT'YAHU 13:22

Why do we fear the future? God is forever sowing the word of His Reign in our hearts... yet the evil one is always trying to take it away. When we do not fully receive that word and make certain it is planted deep inside our minds, it remains superficial pickings for a devouring and ravenous enemy. But sometimes—perhaps often, in fact—it is not the evil one we need to be so worried about. Indeed, our own home-grown worries and anxieties choke out the word that we have already heard... and the evil one is just as pleased for us to steal it from ourselves.

Worry is an anxiety over something that might happen—something we *fear* might happen—even though it also might not. That worrisome thing *might* occur, and it *might* bring with it all the consequences we fear... but it also may never come to pass, and we will have literally worried for nothing. It is the fear of the unknown, then, that we take by the hands, placing them around our own necks. And as the worry squeezes the life out of us, perhaps our last conscious thought will be that, at least, we successfully avoided that which we feared.

As the thorns of anxiety wind their way through our hearts and minds—leaving us immobilized, raw, and unable to think and to feel and to breathe—what will we do, then, should the thing that we fear actually arrive? What clear-thinking action will we be able to take? In what positive direction will we be able to move? What word of God will we be able to hold onto for hope and wisdom and faith? The worry will have killed us—as well as our reliance upon God—long before we ever became infected by the disease.

While we worry and are filled with fear over the unprecedented and the unknown, God knows exactly how everything will unfold, and we have His word to replace our anxiety. Instead of sowing our minds with thoughts that only cultivate our fears, we must take the sickle to our futile attempts at control, and clear the field of our mind so that the word may take root and grow. What is the point of being anxious, since you cannot know or change what is about to happen? Instead, commit your mind to the faith and the knowledge of God, and, no matter what may come, the word in you will be made fruitful for facing the unfathomable future.

PRAYER

Father, how did my hands come to be wrapped around my own throat, rather than gripping relentlessly to Your faithful word? In my anxiety, Abba, I have become my own worst enemy, working the deceiver's deeds upon myself. Help me, Master, to clear the fields of my mind from worry over things that I cannot conceive or control. Be fruitful, ADONAI, and fill my mind with Your word—because, today, Your Reign is the only future I need to know.

NOTHING WILL BE IMPOSSIBLE

> Then the disciples, having come to יֵשׁוּעַ, Yeshua
> *while He was* by Himself, said, "Why were we not
> able to cast him out?" And He said to them, "*It is*
> through your littleness of faith. אָמֵן, Amen, for I
> say to you: if you have faith as a grain of mustard,
> you will *be able to* say to this mountain, 'Move from
> here to there,' and it will move—and nothing will
> be impossible to you." –מַתִּתְיָהוּ MATIT'YAHU 17:19-20

Can your faith literally move a mountain? That doesn't really
seem to make much sense. Believing, hoping and trusting for
the esoteric is one thing, but actually, literally altering the
physical world? And on that kind of scale? It doesn't sound
particularly reasonable. And yet, we ask God for physical healing, for financial assistance, and for changes in our material
circumstances all the time. So why not move a mountain? In
truth, we believe with our whole hearts that if *God* wanted to
move a huge mass of rock and ground whenever and wherever
He pleased, He could certainly do it. After all, He put it there
in the first place. But the idea that *we* can perform such a feat?
That's a lot harder to accept.

And yet, the Master tells us categorically and non-metaphori-
cally that we can literally move mountains. "If you have faith,"
He says, "nothing will be impossible to you." Nothing. But
the reason we don't see God-endorsed faith-changes in our
lives—much less the relocation of mountains—is because
of our "littleness of faith." It's not that we don't have *enough*
faith in terms of allotment; it's that the faith we do have is
considerably underdeveloped.

Our faith, then, needs to be acted upon if it is to ever have any effectiveness. It needs to be exercised. Like any muscle, when it doesn't experience regular use—when we don't work it from time to time for increasingly bigger and greater deeds—it remains small, begins to atrophy, and eventually becomes weak to the point of uselessness. Faith that gives up—that does not press in and endure in the face of difficulty and resistance—can never strengthen and grow. If we only ever try to lift the little things, how can we ever hope to carry the insurmountable?

If you have given up on having faith for things you think are impossible—or even faith for anything at all—take heart, and be renewed in hope! It's time to start working that muscle again, and having faith in God for progressively more and more "impossible" things. If your God is the Maker of mountains—if your Master is the Messiah Yeshua—then your little faith can grow... and move.

PRAYER

ADONAI, my Creator, it feels so impossible to believe for the impossible. I've asked for so many things which didn't come to pass, that I've gotten used to not even asking anymore—in faith, or otherwise. So, Master, please increase my faith—help me to not give up, but to press in, that I may have Your mind and hear Your voice. Help me to learn to distinguish between my wishes and Your will, Abba, as I seek to strengthen my conviction for the unseen. Please show me, awesome God, how to productively exercise my faith in You; teach me to believe You for increasingly bigger and greater things... especially for the impossible!

ON THIS STONE

יֵשׁוּעַ, Yeshua said to them, "Did you never read in the Scriptures, 'A stone that the builders disallowed, it became *the* head of a corner....' and he who is falling on this stone will be broken. And on whomever it falls, it will crush him to pieces."

–מַתִּתְיָהוּ MATIT'YAHU 21:42-44

Are you sure you're following the real Messiah? Of all the people of Israel, the Ko'haniym and P'rushiym should have been the first to recognize who Yeshua truly was. They had all the ancient texts, and access to every prophecy. They were learned, scholarly men—the most devoted to their religion. Surely, they were aware of the messianic signs and qualifications; surely, in Yeshua, they saw the Messiah the world was waiting for.

But just because you spend your life in service to God doesn't mean you'll know Him when you see Him. The Jewish leadership had long been evolving a religion, erecting walls of laws that shrouded the Torah in shadow. What they made (they thought) was a monument to God—a temple of virtue and righteousness. But behind those beautiful barricades, God had gradually become obscured... and it is difficult to later recognize what you've spent your life remaking in your own image.

Like the Ko'haniym and P'rushiym, all who erect their religion over the foundation of God's word will soon know only what their religion tells them. The deeper that foundation is buried—the higher the walls erected around it—the less the light shines on the truth, and the more the darkness penetrates our knowledge. We are fooling ourselves if we think we can daily neglect God's word and still maintain an accurate depiction of Yeshua—the cornerstone—in our hearts and minds. As long as we make the Scriptures a mere monument, they remain closed to us forever.

When the walls of religion fall upon the true cornerstone, all who are in its shadow will be demolished—left in ruin, despair and dismay. Unless we want to one day be broken and crushed by a Messiah we don't even recognize, we must today make the sole source of objective truth—the Scriptures—the only teaching to which we wholly devote ourselves. Being in God's word daily must be a priority for us if we truly want to know the real Messiah. For only through the word of God will we be able to align our lives and identify with the one, true and unobscured cornerstone....

PRAYER

Master Yeshua, I see only You, and today I reject the messiah of my own making. Help me to tear down the walls of religion in my life, Father, that I may find and see You: perfect and unobscured. Align me, ADONAI, with the one, true cornerstone, and let only the weight of Your glory fall on me. Teach me Your ways through Your word, O God, that I may never fail to know You or to follow You, but that I may bring forth the living fruit of Your Reign.

ENTER INTO THE JOY

> "His master said to him, 'Well done, slave, good and faithful! You were faithful over a few things, so now I will set you over many things. Enter into the joy of your master!'" –מַתִּתְיָהוּ MATIT'YAHU 25:21

God has entrusted you with something of great value. It's as wide as the heavens, yet it fits in a hole; it can be held your hand, and yet cover the earth. It can take form and have substance; it can be without any specific shape at all. For each one of us it is distinct, as He gives it to us "according to [our] individual ability" (25:15). But whatever it is, of this we can be sure: it has substantial—and eternal—worth to God.

So now that we possess this thing, He also expects us to use it. He wants us to take it out, put it into action, and unleash its limitless power. And He does not want us to treat it gingerly, but to take risks, and to put it where it has the most potential to expand and grow. We are free to be creative and zealous with whatever form we give it, as long as we don't just keep it to ourselves, or bury it in the ground out of fear.

This thing we have is precious—unique in the universe, valuable beyond all things to which men assign worth. It must not be mishandled or squandered, but it must also not be sequestered—we cannot clutch it so near that no one else gets a chance to grasp it. When the Master returns to see what we have done with His possessions, He won't be pleased with us simply because we didn't misplace what we were given. He will be pleased if we take it out and use it—*often*—and its use results in Him receiving back much more than He initially gave.

What is this thing of great value that God has entrusted to you? What is this thing that morphs in size and influence according to how you treat it? It is Yeshua Himself—or rather, it is you sharing and proclaiming Him according to your individual ability.

If you seek the Master's displeasure, then, by all means, just hoard Him and hide Him in your heart. But if you revere Him and trust Him and desire to enter into His joy, then open your mouth and your hands, and widely invest His truth in the hearts, minds and lives of others. Don't be apprehensive—He's not expecting you to do more than you are able. But now it is time to dig up your treasure. Take some risks with it, and get to work....

PRAYER

ADONAI, my Master, You reap where You do not sow, and gather where You do not scatter. Give me faith, Father, not in my abilities, but in Your ability to use me beyond anything I can ever think of or imagine. I praise Your Name, Yeshua, for You are more precious than anything any man can ever give or possess. Please give me the courage, God, to put to use what You have entrusted to me, that I may be profitable for Your Reign, and You may reap an overabundance in me....

ALWAYS HAVE ME

> And יֵשׁוּעַ, Yeshua, having known *what they were saying*, said to them, "Why do you give trouble to the woman [who poured the expensive ointment on Me]? Indeed, she did a beautiful act for Me; for the poor you *will* always have with you, but you *will* not always have Me." –מַתִּתְיָהוּ MATIT'YAHU 26:11

She came to anoint Him... she did it for His burial. The "beautiful act" of putting ointment on the Master's body was most displeasing to His disciples, as the ointment was "very expensive," and they found the act purposeless and wasteful. Rather than pouring the ointment on Yeshua's head, the disciples felt it would have been better to sell it and give the vast proceeds to the poor. But the Master—eternally kind toward the destitute and impoverished—was having none of it. "Why do you give trouble to the woman?" He chided. "[F]or the poor you *will* always have with you, but you *will* not always have Me."

As deeply as Yeshua cared for the poor, He could not deny the woman her expression of love. There was a growing awareness—even if the disciples were oblivious to it—that the Master would soon be enduring His horrific end, and then going away for good. The poor, He said, would live on; but soon, the disciples would have to care for them without Him. There will always be those who are poor, but there will only ever be one Messiah.

In calling attention to His inevitable departure, what Yeshua spoke was but a prelude to what He would ultimately reveal. Though the Master made it clear how He would soon be leaving them, it would only be in His going away bodily that the world could finally know His eternal presence. Indeed, there will always be those who are poor—not to mention those who are not poverty-stricken, but still lack in wealth and resources. But though the Master is no longer with us physically, we nevertheless "always have [Him]"—and He is the only answer to every need.

As believers in Yeshua, we are exhorted to be compassionate people with a heart for the poor. But we fail those who are less fortunate if we are motivated only to help them materially. The Master's sacrifice meant the end of poverty and lack—if not in this life, then in the next. But no man, woman or child can inherit the promise of His presence if the only salvation they know is for their temporary, physical needs.

What would the world be like if we put half the work into sharing Yeshua that we do toward humanitarian efforts? Yes, let us relieve immediate needs, but not while keeping silent— let us tell them of their need to have Yeshua.

PRAYER

Master, fill my heart with compassion for the poor, but let me give more than just toward their physical need. May my motivation not merely be for charity, but to honor Your sacrifice and to share with them Your eternal habitation. As You accepted a "beautiful" act that might have otherwise blessed the less fortunate, help me to be discerning with the use of my own resources—both materially and spiritually. I praise You, Yeshua, for though You are no longer here, we still have You with us… always.

NOT AS I WILL

> Then [Yeshua] said to them, "Exceedingly sorrowful is My soul—to death. Remain here and *stay* awake with Me." And having gone forward a little, He fell on His face, praying and saying, "My Father! If it is possible, let this cup pass from Me! Nevertheless, not as I will, but as You *will*."
> —מַתִּתְיָהוּ MATIT'YAHU 26:38-39

The Master Yeshua, full of anguish and sorrow, was knowingly facing His execution. Not even His closest friends had the physical or spiritual fortitude to comfort Him. He was completely alone. Confronting the climax of His entire reason for being, our powerful Master—the Son of God—then made His desperate appeal: Is there any way I can avoid what's in front of me? Please, Father, don't make me go through with this!

His heart laid bare, His deepest feelings spoken aloud, the Messiah then did for us one of the greatest things He would ever do: He bowed His wants and His hopes to those of the Father—He submitted Himself and surrendered His circumstances to the Father's will.

Not one of us will ever even come close to dying under the weight of the world's sin. Indeed, we cannot even bear the torturous weight of our own. How much more, then, should we strive to follow the Master's example, not only as we face hardship and pain, but as we conduct ourselves in our normal, everyday lives. How much more should we continually surrender our will to the Master's.

The Father has His plans for us, and often, they will involve excruciating things we desperately don't want to do. Will we then turn our backs on Him in the hopes of finding a more palatable way? Or will we follow the Master's example, surrender our dreams and desires, and fully submit our will to our loving Father?

When we avoid God's plans, we miss His purpose. When we set aside ourselves, we find the fullness of who we were meant to be. "Not as I will, but as You *will*," my God....

PRAYER

I bless Your Name, ADONAI; please forgive me for trying to make my own plans without You. Help me to reach Your destiny for me, even if I must first pass through deep anguish and despair. As Your Son laid down His life for mine, Father, I now surrender all of my wants and circumstances, and submit my will totally to Yours. I trust You, O God, to lead me according to Your perfect plan. I humbly lay myself down, and follow...

HE WILL NOT ABANDON YOU

> [A]nd those passing by *there* were speaking evil of Him, wagging their heads [and saying,] "He saved others, *but* he is not able to save himself! He is *the* King of יִשְׂרָאֵל, Yis'rael! Let him come down now from the stake, and we will believe in him! [And] about the ninth hour, יֵשׁוּעַ, Yeshua cried out with a loud voice, saying, "אֵלִי אֵלִי לָמָה עֲזַבְתָּנִי, Eliy! Eliy! Lamah 'azav'taniy?"—that is, "MY GOD! MY GOD! WHY DID YOU ABANDON ME?" [And] יֵשׁוּעַ, Yeshua, having shouted again with a loud voice, yielded the רוּחַ, ruach.
>
> –מַתִּתְיָהוּ MATIT'YAHU 27:39, 42, 46, 50

Under the crushing weight of the sin of the world, the Messiah cried out with a loud voice—a voice of agony and helplessness. His mockers were right: as the Son of God, He could have come down at any time from His execution stake. But instead, He made the same decision over and over again—moment by moment, pain after pain—to stay there... for us.

Our Master did not endure that extreme torture and anguish just because it was the necessary path that would lead to our salvation from death. He remained there, choosing the asphyxiating, flesh-tearing experience on our behalf, so that He could feel it, so that He could know it, and so that He could become the way out—the way through—for our own agonies of life... large or small.

No matter what you have suffered, or what you are going through now, the Master Yeshua literally and fully understands. He has taken upon Himself your misery, your pain, your anguish, your agony, your questioning of God's plans, your feelings of being abandoned and rejected… your sin. He has felt what you feel; He has carried the weight you bear.

Every time you are feeling forgotten and deserted—whenever you are being crushed under the weight and uncertainties of life—look to the execution stake of Messiah. See the Master in all His grisly suffering and remember the painful choice He made: that in the middle of His asking if God had left *Him* alone, Yeshua stayed there… until the end… for you.

PRAYER

O Yeshua, how You love me and gave Yourself for me! Forgive me of my sins, and for foolishly thinking that my suffering could ever even approach what You have suffered for me. Thank You for Your eternal hope and salvation, my Master; thank You for never leaving me alone. I praise You, Yeshua— my Redeemer, my Savior, my friend… faithful until the end.

HAVING SEEN THE EARTHQUAKE

> And the centurion and those watching יֵשׁוּעַ,
> Yeshua with him, having seen the earthquake
> and the things that were done, were exceeding-
> ly afraid, saying, "Truly, this was God's Son."
> –מַתִּתְיָהוּ MATIT'YAHU 27:54

"Did you hear? They finally caught that kook who said he
would destroy the Temple and then rebuild it in three days!
Yeah, he claims he's some kind of time-traveler or something—
that he was alive before Abraham was. Can you believe that!
What did you say? Now he thinks he's the King of the Jews?
Oh, sure. And I'm the Queen of Sheba. Next thing you know
he'll be performing 'miracles' and telling people their sins are
forgiven. Are you kidding me? He actually did that? Okay.
And I've got a bridge in the Kidron Valley to sell you. Say
again? He's the Messiah of Israel? The Son of God? What a
joke! Listen, you'd have to rip the Temple curtain in half from
top to bottom with an earthquake and crack open the tombs
in Jerusalem before I'd believe anything as wacky as that!"

For years the Master had been walking the streets of Jerusalem, touring the countryside of Israel and teaching the word
of God in the Temple. He had been laying hands on the sick,
performing miraculous feats before thousands, and binding
up the broken in both heart and spirit. His practical ministry
was not a mystery, though His message was perplexing at
times. But inaccessible? No. Out of reach? Hardly. For those
who sought to know Him and find salvation for their souls,
Yeshua was right there—totally available—and possible to be
believed in.

As "the centurion and those watching עִשׂוּ, Yeshua with him" stood there, observing the savior of the world succumb to His undeserved sentence, they had all heard the rumors—mixed with facts—and wondered who He truly was. Had they followed Him, learned from Him, and sought out the truth, they would have seen and heard for themselves, and been confident in knowing what He said. Yet it would take the Master's gory death, accompanied by a seismic upheaval of biblical proportions, to shake out their doubt and disbelief. They needed a jolt of otherworldly reality before they could see and confess that "Truly, this was God's Son."

Is your walk with Yeshua based only on rumor and innuendo? Have you been relying too heavily on the knowledge base of others? Don't wait to learn of Him for yourself until it's too late to follow Him any further. Don't wait, such that the coming revelation of God strikes fear in your heart. He is not inaccessible; He is not unavailable. Pursue Him through His word, and get to know Him firsthand. It should not take an earthquake to get you to understand.

PRAYER

Master Yeshua, I have been blind. I have been accepting at face value what others have been teaching me about You, rather than verifying the truth for myself. Forgive me, Father, for walking with a version of You based on hearsay, when I should have been gaining firsthand knowledge daily by Your word. ADONAI—Shaker of earth and men—awaken my mind, that I may fully follow the real You. I praise You, Yeshua, Savior of my soul—truly, You are the Son of God!

WITH YOU

"And look! I am with you all the days—until the full end of the age!" –מַתִּתְיָהוּ MATIT'YAHU 28:18-20)

As the Master prepared for His inevitable ascension, He gave His disciples their final instructions—but not without words of comfort. The road before them would be arduous and paved with persecution, but they had His assurance that no matter what trial or oppression they would endure in His Name, He would be with them. Though they would see Him again after this for only a little while, the disciples would nevertheless carry on in His Name for the rest of their lives, despite His physical absence. For them, the Master's assurance was more than enough. They had seen the miraculous—witnessed the power of God—such that they could confidently take Yeshua at His word.

Our lives, on the other hand, are often so busy and full that we never even think about "God with us," much less the Life that is to come. We have jobs and families and bills and any number of things right now that weigh on us, keeping us overly-focused on today—to the exclusion of almost everything else. This obsession leaves us susceptible not only to feelings of loneliness and vulnerability, but also to arrogance, causing us to act as if we can successfully navigate life without God's active guidance. And, of course—whether we ever come to realize it or not—we can't.

But just like Yeshua's first, faithful disciples, we too can walk in the full confidence of His presence in our daily lives—as long as we aren't fixated on today. While there is no denying that our present busyness and obstacles and difficulties are real, our reality in Messiah is instead bound to "the full end of the age." His presence in our daily trials *and even our joys* is not limited whatsoever by His physical absence. No matter what we think, or what it may sometimes feel like, we are *not* alone.

Until the day that we go home to be with Yeshua forever, for as long as we know Him and follow Him and give Him our lives, we too have that same assurance—that He is with us *now*. Take comfort and find strength in knowing that Yeshua is truly present in your life now and forever—that no matter what circumstances life may bring, He is already there to meet them... *with you....*

PRAYER

Yeshua, I praise Your Name, and commit my life to Your awesome service. Thank You, Master, that You are with me *now*, and that there is no road in life I will ever be forced to take without You. Help me, O God, to not forget the enduring presence of Your Son—that I will see Him at work in my life, even though He is unseeable. I praise You, Yeshua, ever present Savior—eternal Master of all of my todays....

SO THAT YOU MAY BE HEALED

> So be confessing *your* sins to one another, and be
> praying for one another, *so* that you may be healed…
> —בַּיַעֲקֹב YAʾAQOV 5:16A

When was the last time you confessed your sins—to a person?
When was the last time you even realized that you still commit
them? In today's Body of Messiah, not only is it rare that we
come clean with a fellow-believer about things we've recently
done (or thought), but we are also not taught to be self-aware,
and to reflect on our own behavior and thought-life. At least,
not in terms of *sin*. And, ironically, in an age when we publish
our entire personal lives all over the internet, we as followers of Yeshua are also conditioned to keep the *really* private,
embarrassing, shameful stuff to ourselves.

So if we're oblivious to—or hiding, or simply ignoring—our
sins, how can we confess them to one another? And if we don't
confess them to one another, then how can we pray for one
another? And if we can't pray for one another, then how can
we be healed?—healed of our sicknesses and diseases… healed
from the effects of our sin.

Somewhere along the way, we as a Body began to stigmatize
shame to such an extent that no one feels it is either safe or
necessary to tell others about our sins. We think that it is
enough to confess them to God, or, if we are not going to
confess them openly to Him, it is enough that we know that
He knows. The confession of sin was never for the purpose of
passing judgment or holding others hostage with their secrets.
We are supposed to confess our sins in order to lift the shame,
and as a peer-pressure deterrent against future sin.

As the Body of Messiah, we are long overdue to reject the private independence that keeps us separated from one another, even when we are gathered together. We need to cultivate relationships of mutual trust, interest, respect and love founded on our shared faith in Messiah; we need to break through our own walls of inhibition and fear, and recognize that God's work in our lives is meant to be done also through others—for the sanctification of all.

So today, prepare your heart, and take a good, hard look at your deepest you. Acknowledge your sins first to yourself, and then confess them, receive prayer, and be healed.

PRAYER

Abba, Father, it is so hard to take that inward look, because I already know what I'm going to see. Help me to remember that You aren't just waiting around, looking for an excuse to strike me down, but that Your desire is for me to be healed— unburdened of my sin and shame. Give me the courage to obey Your word, Master, and seek out mature, trustworthy fellow-believers with whom I can confess my sins. I praise You, Yeshua, that through the members of Your Body, You will do Your healing work in me...

THE TORAH, PROVIDED

> But the goal of this mandate is love out of a pure heart, and of a good conscience, and of faith unfeigned, from which certain *men*, having swerved, turned aside to fruitless discussion, wanting to be teachers of תּוֹרָה, Torah, not understanding either the things they say, nor regarding what they confidently assert. Rather, we have known that the תּוֹרָה, Torah *is* good, provided one uses it lawfully....
>
> –1 TIMOTHY 1:5-8

The word of God is life, and His Torah—a delight. Those who walk in its ways are blameless; those who fix their eyes on its commands will not be put to shame. Though many, lacking understanding, think the Torah is heavy-handed and a burden, in actuality its commands are holy, righteous and good (Romans 7:12). Yet some of us, in our zeal, find the Torah to be *so* righteous and *so* good that we feel it necessary to militantly advance it upon others. At the expense of faith, love and the stewardship of God, we make the glorious Torah a weighty weapon.

This peculiar phenomenon—having affected some of us in the Body of Messiah—while hardly new, should not come as a surprise. Such will always be the result when we venerate our own thoughts and ideas under the guise of following the word of God. No one with sincere motives sets out to do this, of course, but sometimes we will cause this very good Torah to loom so large in our eyes that we begin to mistake it for something else—and our zeal turns into fanaticism. This use of the Torah is what the Scriptures call "unlawful," and it warps the perfect Torah into something abusive, and not very good at all.

The "lawful" use of the Torah, then, is not found in endless debate and combative "teaching," but in identifying and addressing *sin*. The goal of Torah was *never* Torah-keeping itself, but rather the Messiah, and "love out of a pure heart, and of a good conscience, and of faith unfeigned." But when our love for the true purpose of the Torah is twisted to become love for "fruitless discussion" and for "wanting to be teachers of תּוֹרָה, Torah" and for being on a crusade to get everyone else to keep Torah, then we have "swerved [and] turned aside"—not just from our faith, but from the true Torah itself.

Yes, the Torah is very, very good, but *only* if we use it "lawfully"—for we have the power to misuse and pervert it. Be careful with how you regard the Torah—indeed, the whole word of God—and the spirit in which you promote it to others. Don't let overzealousness and a misplaced love make the word of God into something far less than good....

PRAYER

Father, Your word is holy, and Your Torah is true and good! Please bring understanding to my mind about how I have been misusing and mistreating Your word, ADONAI, that I may truly know its good and lawful purpose in my life and the lives of others. Make me pure of heart, Master—my faith both genuine and sincere. Temper in me, O God, any overzealousness for and unhealthy fixation upon Your Torah—temper it with the life-giving power of Your great, good love.

A TRANQUIL AND PEACEABLE LIFE

> I exhort *you*, then, first of all, *that* there be made requests for help, prayers, petitions, *and* thanksgivings for all men... so that we may lead a tranquil and peaceable life in all godliness and seriousness. This *is* right and acceptable in the sight of God our Savior, who wants all men to be saved, and to come to the full knowledge of the truth.
>
> –1 Timothy 2:1-4

What angers or concerns you the most? Political and social division? The insane rhetoric and doublespeak? The systematic undermining of religious liberty? The flagrant disregard for due process and freedom of speech? The continued slaughter of innocent babies in the womb—and the deranged celebration of it? Whatever it is, you're not alone. "Divided" is indeed an appropriate word to describe our world today. Another one is "hostile." So other than taking sides, defending or advancing our positions, and screaming at each other across the chasm between us, what else are we supposed to do?

"I exhort *you*, then, first of all, *that* there be made requests for help, prayers, petitions, *and* thanksgivings for all men...."

When life, liberty, safety and security are on the line, surely there will be a time for heated debate, aggressive protest, and everything that goes along with them. And yes, perhaps by political, legal or physical force we can achieve "a tranquil and peaceable life"—for a season. But there is really only one thing that will bring about lasting peace and tranquility, both in this life and the next, and that is salvation through our

Master, the Messiah Yeshua. Only when we have Yeshua and the word of God in common with each other will we even have a chance at finding common ground on any issue—least of all, the most divisive.

The most important thing we can do to bring healing and peace to our world is to pray for *everyone*—especially those we perceive as our enemies—and to act in accordance with those prayers, that they may be saved and come to the full knowledge of the truth. We must step back from our own fury and fiery speech, and see our opponents through God's eyes: as creatures specially made in His image, with whom He desires above all things to be reconciled.

If we cannot bring ourselves to pray for the salvation of those who would rob us of our way of life—those who would make criminal the exercise of our God-given rights, those who would murder the most innocent among us—then we are just as much a part of the problem as they are. If we will not see past our own issues and anger and rhetoric—if we refuse to see our opponents as the Creator Himself made them—then perhaps we too are perpetuating the fight, and needing to come to the full knowledge of the truth....

PRAYER

Abba, Father, it is right and acceptable in Your sight that *all people* may be saved, even and especially those toward whom I have hatred in my heart. Forgive me, Master, for forgetting that You are the only true solution to the world's problems, and that all my words and actions in defense of the truth are nothing without Your kindness and love. Soften my heart, Abba, and fill me with Your compassion, that *my* prayers will be the ones that bring Your lonely, lost ones home...

PAY CLOSE ATTENTION

> Let no one despise your youth; but in word, in behavior, in love, in faith, *and* in purity, become a pattern for those believing.... Pay close attention to yourself and to the teaching; remain in them, for *by* doing this thing, you will save both yourself and those hearing you. –1 TIMOTHY 4:16

Timothy had his work cut out for him. Paul had left him behind in Ephesus to continue the work of the Good News, but at a disadvantage. While Paul was an educated man of status, which carried with it an air of authority, Timothy was just... young. Surely Paul had confidence in Timothy—enough to leave the Called-Forth community of Ephesus to his care. Yet Timothy's age was an inescapable liability. Paul was concerned that many there in Ephesus would "despise [his] youth"—and he exhorted Timothy to not allow that to happen.

It was up to him, then, to "become a pattern for those believing." If Timothy wanted the people there to take him seriously, he needed to rise above his disadvantage and be someone no one could legitimately fault or reject. To accomplish this, Paul encouraged him to be an example "in word, in behavior, in love, in faith, *and* in purity," and to "pay attention to the reading, to the exhortation, *and* to the teaching" (4:13). But all these would be undermined if Timothy did not take care to do perhaps the most important thing of all. Paul said to Timothy, "Pay close attention to yourself... for *by* doing this thing, you will save both yourself and those hearing you."

As is the case for us all, Timothy would be unable to exemplify the Messiah without conducting a continuous examination of himself. Paul knew that in order for Timothy to become a pattern that people would want to emulate, he could not simply perform his various functions, hoping—or imagining—that he was fulfilling those lofty characteristics and behaviors. Rather, Timothy needed to "pay close attention" to himself to ensure that he was actually living up to the example he was trying to set. Indeed, how could he expect to sufficiently represent Yeshua if he was oblivious to his own behavior?

Like Timothy, we all have some kind of disadvantage when it comes to being effective examples of Messiah. Because people will always look for a reason in us to discount our words and our testimony, we too must remain vigilant in our attitudes and actions. Don't be averse to self-examination to make sure your rhetoric and your reactions are lining up with the pure word of God. Take care not to give others unnecessary cause to despise you—take responsibility for your behavior, and "pay close attention to yourself."

PRAYER

Master Yeshua, I praise Your awesome and mighty Name— help me to be worthy to carry it. Show me, God, how my attitudes and actions have been undermining and compromising who I truly am in You. Teach me, ADONAI, how to effectively evaluate myself, that I may correct my behavior and line myself up fully with Your word. Make me a humble pattern of You for others to emulate, Master; make me see myself clearly... and pay attention.

IT IS GREAT GAIN

> But it is great gain—the godliness *that comes* with contentment! For we brought nothing into the world, since we are able to carry nothing out. But having food and clothing—with these we will be content. – I TIMOTHY 6:6-8

How could it ever be wrong to desire closeness with God?—to want to reflect His character?—to be a godly person? On its face, godliness should be one of the more obvious and commendable character traits we seek, following the pattern of the Master Yeshua, who only did what He saw the Father doing.

But what if we started using that character trait to our own advantage? What if we could find a way to exploit our godliness for selfish gain—to peddle it as a commodity—even to profit from it financially? Sounds crazy, right? The concept doesn't even make any sense. And yet, according to the Scriptures, certain ones have strayed from the "teaching according to godliness" (6:3). Possessing an inflated sense of self, they have become "wholly corrupted in mind and destitute of the truth, supposing the godliness to be *a means of* gain" (6:5).

Thankfully, there is indeed great gain to be had from godliness, and we should desire it in extravagant excess. That gain, however, is not simply from any form of "godliness," but rather, "the godliness *that comes* with contentment!" True godliness, then, is not able to be tempted by either wealth or want. Rather, true godliness comes from contentment with what we already have—humbly realizing that we brought nothing into the world, nor will we carry anything out—and simply being satisfied with that.

Godliness without contentment gains us nothing but the desire for more gain. Instead, let us be content not because of status or money or financial sufficiency, but because of Messiah—and have a genuine satisfaction with the level of life and wealth with which He has already blessed us.

"Having food and clothing," then, and closeness to our God... with these let us be content.

PRAYER

Abba, Father, how I desire to be close to You, to live like Your Son, and to be pure in godliness. Keep me from perverting that godliness through a false perception of myself, and of the value I place on wealth and the things I think I need. Instead, help me to value the life You have given me just the way it is. ADONAI, change my heart to find contentment where I have previously lusted and longed for more. Teach me, Master, to find my real worth, my true value, and my fulfillment only in You...

BRING YOURSELF NEAR

> Be diligent to bring yourself near—proven to God,
> a workman irreproachable, straightly cutting *a path*
> for the word of the truth.... –2 TIMOTHY 2:15

Do you feel unworthy to approach God? Perhaps it's because of your sense of humility—indeed, who could ever be deserving of coming near to their Creator? Or maybe it's that you feel guilty because, deep down, you know that the old you is still in there somewhere... and maybe not so old after all. But these ideas betray the fundamental truth of how God sees you, now that you are in Messiah. He has made you clean, and you are therefore worthy of entering into God's presence.

That feeling of unworthiness, then, comes from the awareness of how we regularly sully that pure gift when we continue to sin. We realize that we have been careless—thoughtless— neglecting our new creation, and staining what God has made immaculate. So we retreat into ourselves and revert to old patterns and ways, as we create distance from God in our shame. Our words, attitudes and behavior toward others become misaligned with who we are in Messiah, and we mar the reputation of our Master while obscuring the word of truth from view.

But as much as the choice to sin remains an option for us, so does the choice to seek forgiveness. And not only does that forgiveness remain available to us—despite what we continue to do—we owe it to our Master to ask for it, so that we may restore both our condition and His honor. No matter what wrong we commit, we still have a responsibility—especially in front of those who do not yet know Him—to make the path to Yeshua and His word clear, straight and unobstructed. We should be blameless and irreproachable, both in word and in deed, as a flawless testimony of the life-changing salvation of our God.

Be diligent, then, to bring yourself near to God—the One who remains faithful even when we are not. Then, in your words and your ways, prove the work He has done in you, that you may never be a hindrance, but always a faithful workman clearing a pathway for the perfect word of His truth....

PRAYER

Adonai my God, were it not for the sacrifice of Your Son, I would be wholly unworthy of Your presence and Your Name! Forgive me, Father, for walking in crooked ways, when I should have been straightly following Your word of truth. Help me, Master, to diligently bring myself near to You, that I may completely disavow my fleshly ways. Make me a workman irreproachable, untiringly cutting a straight path, so that others, too, may come near to You....

EVERY SCRIPTURE

> Every Scripture *is* God-breathed, and profitable...
> – 2 Timothy 3:16a

Do you believe that all Scripture—every Scripture—is God-breathed? It hardly seems likely, doesn't it? Surely, while men had it in their hands, God let them slip through a word or two of their own. Perhaps, in between Adonai's heavenly breaths, those wordsmiths managed to even squeeze in some completely original thoughts—perhaps an entire doctrine! Maybe the whole thing is just made up, and we're all just a bunch of deluded fools for paying any attention to it. Fiction and fables; babble and baloney. Come on—we're smarter than that.

This is the slippery slope that we inevitably put ourselves on every time we mishandle the Scriptures—when we try to make it say what we want it to say; when we reject the plain sense of the text because it doesn't line up with other "truth" we think we know. But God did not give us the Scriptures simply so that we could know the truth. He also gave them to us so that we could confidently refute and rebuke other believers who will not "tolerate the sound teaching" and who "heap up teachers to themselves" (4:3)—teachers who will tell them exactly what they want to hear.

No one will own up to this, of course—surely, it's impossible that we ourselves might be those very misguided believers or false teachers. Indeed, we will say that it is everyone else who is wrong, and we can prove it from the word. So we string together contextually unrelated terms and verses, connecting them with a web of equivocations and logic based on faulty, untenable premises. And it is here, as we assert our own authority, rationale and luminosity, that we deny the true source of God's word. We twist the Scriptures "according to [our] own lusts" (4:3), having turned aside from the truth.

The Scriptures are supposed to be the one thing we as followers of Yeshua are unable to argue about. Instead, all too often we fail to genuinely assign them the weight and authority they deserve as the sole arbiter of faith that they truly are. The sad reality for us as believers in Yeshua is that we *don't* all really believe that the Scriptures are God-breathed and, therefore, out of reach of man's interpretations. So we continue to debate and disagree, considering ourselves enlightened despite our collective deception, weakness and disunity.

Everything you believe, say, and do depends upon how you view the Scriptures. It's time for you to decide whose words you believe they really are:

God's? Or man's?...

...because they can't be both.

PRAYER

ADONAI, Your Scriptures are perfect and true; Your word is sufficient and supreme! Forgive me for trying to assert my own ideas and authority—or somebody else's—over Your solely God-breathed word. Humble me, Master, and open my eyes to where I have rejected Your sound and perfect direction. Teach me, refute me, set me aright, and instruct me only in Your righteousness....

ALWAYS BE READY

> And always BE ready for *making a verbal* defense to everyone who is asking you for an account regarding the hope that IS in you, but with humility and fear, having a good conscience, so that in that in which they speak against you, they may be ashamed—*those* who are defaming your good behavior in Messiah. –כֵּיפָא א 1 KEIFA 3:15B-16

Do you feel persecuted for being a believer in Messiah? The idea is ridiculous, of course, given the literal danger and oppression some believers around the world face today—not to mention the real suffering and persecution that the disciples of Yeshua's generation endured. But even though you and I aren't actually being persecuted as Scripture depicts persecution (yet!), we're certainly hated and reviled. Some of us are even made to suffer—emotionally, financially, in our reputations, or in our way of life. No doubt, there are people in our society who would love to see us hurt, even dead, and are happy to hurl such sentiments our way.

So how did God's enemies become so emboldened? How did normal, everyday people come to despise the message of love, hope, forgiveness and salvation? It happened because we as Messiah's Body have grown increasingly unprepared to make *"a verbal defense* to everyone... regarding the hope" that we have in Yeshua. In this generation especially, we have been trained to focus on our feelings and the conservation of our comfort, rather than on self-sacrifice and the willingness to suffer for the sake of righteousness. But more than that, we have been untrained in the fundamentals of our faith, and how to effectively form a verbal response when that faith is questioned or defamed.

When we open our mouths to speak the truth of Messiah—to defend both His Name and our "good behavior"—it is to bring shame to our detractors. The light is meant to expose the ugly heart that needs eternal healing. But when we do not proclaim God's goodness and hope—and worse, neglect to stand up for it—the only shame we bring is upon ourselves. To fail to put up a defense of our Savior and His word is to strengthen the boldness of our adversaries.

The time is coming—and even now has come—when you will need to speak up and declare the hope of the Messiah to ears that do not want to hear. Will you shrink back in self-love and cede more ground to those who hate you? Or, in selfless love, will you make a legitimate defense of your faith and uphold the reputation of your God?

So what will it be? Retreat? Or give an answer? Which one are you most ready—and most likely—to do?

PRAYER

Father, I confess today my apprehension and fear where it comes to verbally defending my faith in You. Forgive me, Master, for being so unfamiliar with the basic truth of Your word that I feel unprepared to speak up in love for Your advancement or in Your defense. Fill me with courage, ADONAI, and the power of Your Ruach—but more than that, let me not be lacking in knowledge. Drive me to Your word, O God; implant it deep inside me, and make me ready to stand and be silent no more...

HAVING CAST ALL YOUR CARE

> [C]lothe yourselves with humble-mindedness, be-
> cause GOD RESISTS THE PROUD, BUT TO
> THE HUMBLE HE GIVES *UNMERITED*
> FAVOR. Be humbled, then, under the powerful
> hand of God, so that He may exalt you in good
> time, having cast all your care on Him, because
> He cares for you. –כֵּיפָא א 1 KEIFA 5:5B-7

What do you do with all your worries, anxieties and concerns? Do you hold on to them, trying to handle things on your own? Or do you just ignore them—or imagine you're ignoring them—as you bury them deep down inside, hoping to never see them again? Maybe you attempt to exert some level of control over your life, even when everything is completely out of your hands. However you deal with things, of this you can be certain: you're doing it totally wrong... as long as you're not giving it *all* to God.

Worry is actually quite the self-centered thing. It swaddles you, ironically providing a false sense of security as it wraps you up in its warm cocoon of plans, strategies and worst-case scenarios. It makes you believe in the truly unbelievable—that you somehow possess the power to control the uncontrollable. But in reality, worry only empowers you to think far more of yourself and your own capabilities than you ought. And, in the end, it serves to finally weigh you down, undermine your faith, and eat you up from the inside out.

When you worry, it means you have forgotten that God still sees you—and, most importantly, that He still cares. Your anxiety claims an authority that it no longer holds, as it expresses a concern for and attention toward your needs that you mistakenly think belongs to you alone. When you fail to "cast all your care on" God, you are not only fomenting your own misery, but you are actually robbing yourself of the opportunity for God to unburden your heart and mind. But more than that, your worrying subverts God's authority over you—you're not just holding on to your cares and concerns... you're holding on to your *pride*.

Whatever cares you're still carrying today, God is ready and willing to take them away. All you have to do is humble yourself, demolish your pride, and relinquish control of your circumstances, your heart, and your mind. As long as you keep trying to bear your burdens all by yourself, no one else can carry them for you. God's powerful hands are ready to catch every last care you throw at Him, because—simply— "He cares for you."

PRAYER

Father, I have been holding on for dear life to my worries, anxieties and concerns; please forgive me for not remembering to give them all to You. Break me and humble me, my Master, that I may be unburdened of this weight, and joyfully receive Your unmerited favor. I praise You, ADONAI, for You are not too big or too busy to take on even my tiniest of cares. I cast them all upon You, O God, and renounce all control. Thank You, Abba, for loving and caring for me...

SO THAT NONE OF YOU MAY BE HARDENED

> Rather, exhort one another every day—while *it* is called the Today—so that none of you may be hardened by the deceitfulness of the sin. For we have become sharers of the Messiah if *to* the beginning of the confidence we hold fast until the end.... –עִבְרִים Iv'riym 3:13-14

How confident are you in God? Do you trust Him? Are you convinced that He hears your prayers? Do you believe He has your best interests in mind? Or are you following Him grudgingly—like Israel did for 40 years in the desert—provoking Him, ungrateful, in disbelief, not realizing the treasure you have in Him, and going astray in your heart? Is God really there, or not?

As we face difficulties, sadness, disappointment and hardship, we become vulnerable to such hardening. Given enough time and distraction, we will begin to believe our own inner propaganda that help is not on its way—that we are truly on our own. That is why we are very clearly warned: if we do not actively and consistently trust in God, as Israel failed to do (3:7-11), then "there will be in any *one* of you an evil heart of unbelief *resulting* in the falling away from the living God" (3:12).

This isn't a threat, by the way—it's a fact. If we harden our hearts toward God, it will result in unbelief and our falling away from Him! Surely, you don't wish such an end for yourself, or for your fellow followers of Messiah. What, then, must you do? How do you resist the unbelief spreading in your heart? You need to lift up your head, emerge from your self-oriented world, and *daily* reach out to other believers in encouragement and exhortation. Not a day should go by without exhorting someone else, so that none of us may be hardened by the deceitfulness of sin. When we exhort one another, we are engaging our belief in God—reminding ourselves that He is real, and true, and present, and faithful to us... His children.

So, wake up, my brother, my sister! Do not harden your heart! Hold fast to your confidence in God! Keep your eyes fixed on Him! He has not forgotten you; rather, He is standing with you! Do not worry about what your eyes cannot see, for God sees—and that is enough. Just soften your heart, remember His word, and trust that He is always—faithfully—here.

PRAYER

ADONAI, I praise and bless You, for You have always walked with me, even in my wandering. Lead me, Father, and protect me in my troubles; I trust in Your guiding hand. Wake me up, O God, that I may see and recall Your salvation, and then cause me to lift up Your Name in exhortation, so that none of Your children may be hardened and fall away. Thank You, Abba, for softening my heart... now help me to keep walking with faith.

IN ALL THINGS LIKEWISE

> Having, then, a great כֹּהֵן גָּדוֹל, Kohen Gadol passed through the heavens—יֵשׁוּעַ, Yeshua, the Son of God—let us hold fast *to* the profession *of faith.* For we have a כֹּהֵן גָּדוֹל, Kohen Gadol not unable to sympathize with our weaknesses, but ONE tempted in all things likewise *as we are, yet remaining* apart from sin. –עִבְרִים Iv'riym 4:14-15

Do you realize that Yeshua is just like us? In many respects, we tend to forget that our Master—the Messiah, the Word, the Son of God—walked this earth, and ascended to Heaven, as a man. Acknowledging this does not deduct from His deity whatsoever, but forgetting such truth actually keeps us at a distance from God.

It should bring us great comfort that he calls us "brothers" (2:11), and "seeing [that] the children have shared in blood and flesh, He Himself likewise shared of the same" (2:14). In other words, He is human, like us. And He shared in our physical nature for a very specific purpose: "so that through [His] death He might destroy him *who is* having the power of death" (2:14), and therefore deliver us. This is why "it was necessary *for* Him to be made like the brothers in all things" (2:17)—and this is where it starts to really challenge our preconceptions. Because in being made like us "in all things," Yeshua was also "tempted in all things likewise *as we are.*"

And this should give us the greatest hope of all! If He is like us "in all things," and He was tempted like us "in all things," then we know that anything with which we are tempted can be fully resisted and overcome. Why? Because our Master—a temptable human being just like us—nevertheless remained "apart from sin." Indeed, since He "Himself [was] tempted"—and unless it was real temptation, His sympathy is a lie—He is now "able to help those who are tempted" (2:18). We... are not... alone!

In our daily walk with Yeshua, focusing on His humanity as equally as His deity will give us confidence and hope. Though we are not exactly like Yeshua in every way, our humanity is just like His, and therefore so is the way we are able to respond to temptation. Yeshua's tempted yet sinless example is not unattainable for us. Rather, we can strive for it, reach out for it, and hold fast to it whenever we need it the most. "Let us come near, then—unhindered—to the throne of *unmerited* favor, so that we may receive *loving*-kindness and find *unmerited* favor—for timely help" (4:16).

PRAYER

O Yeshua, as I draw near to You, help me to see and accept Your perfect humanity. Teach me to understand Your example not as an impossible standard that only God could achieve, but as a realistic path that You passed through the very heavens to make for me. Fill me with hope and confidence, Master, that Your ability to resist temptation is not unattainable to me, and that I too may remain "apart from sin." Thank You, Father, that "in all [human] things" You made Your perfect, heavenly and holy Son just like me...

FORGIVENESS COMES

> And with blood, almost all things are purified according to the תּוֹרָה, Torah; and apart from blood-shedding, forgiveness does not come.
> —עִבְרִים Iv'riym 9:22

Do you consider yourself to be a good person? In general, do you think you tend to do the right thing? If there's an afterlife, and if there's a heaven and a hell, and if there's a Judge who will pass judgment on you, do you believe, overall, you will be judged "good"?

But what if you've ever done anything bad… *ever*—something wrong against another person? What if you've lied, or lashed out in anger, or had lustful thoughts about someone, or taken something that wasn't yours… or worse? But what if you sought forgiveness from the people you wronged? And what if you actually received that forgiveness from them?

Would you be surprised, then, to find out that the balance of your "good" life, and the forgiveness from people you wronged, is not enough to erase the stains on your record?— that you will *not* be judged "good," but, in fact, deserving of a death sentence?

Sounds extremely unfair, doesn't it? It feels unjust that the good things you've done and the fences you've mended aren't taken into account. But that's just because we don't know—or don't accept—the rules. Such harsh judgment would only be unfair if the rules didn't provide an alternate remedy. Thankfully, they do, and it will only cost you… your life.

The price for forgiveness is the shedding of blood, which means someone is going to die for what you've done. No matter how many laws you haven't broken, it can't make up for the ones you have, and the cost of clemency is death. If only someone else could pay it…

The Good News is that the Messiah Yeshua has already defeated death, and His blood can more than cover your debt. Choose to follow Yeshua, and He will take your place—your life will belong to Him, and you will receive complete forgiveness. Either you pay the price, or He does. Those are the rules.

Maybe giving your life to Yeshua in exchange for salvation doesn't seem quite fair. But then, who are you to judge?

PRAYER

Master Yeshua, I have sinned, and I see my need for forgiveness. I accept Your terms of ownership over myself and receive the gift of eternal life that You bought through Your death and rising again. Thank You, God, Judge over all, for accepting the blood of Your Son where mine is deserved. You are just, compassionate, and full of unmerited favor, ADONAI; You alone are good.

A CONFIDENCE OF
THINGS HOPED FOR

> Now faith is a confidence of things hoped for,
> a conviction regarding matters not seen....
> –עִבְרִים Iv'riym 11:1

How sure are you of Yeshua's return? You never saw Him in the flesh. You didn't witness His powerful acts. You didn't walk with Him, eat with Him, or speak with Him. You didn't watch Him die, and then see Him alive again and ascend to Heaven. You have no first-hand evidence He ever even existed. How strongly can you truly believe in things you have never seen?

Some may say we are deluded or misled, ignorant or irrational. They will say that faith denies reality and reason. But real belief is none of these things. It is neither random, blind nor baseless. Rather, true faith is bold, deliberate, reasonable and firmly rooted... in hope.

Now, hope can be a tricky thing. We may think we're hoping when all we're actually doing is wishing—simply wanting—which isn't grounded in anything. True hope, then, requires *confidence* that what we are waiting for will one day be. It necessitates an internal *conviction* that regardless of what we do or do not see today, the invisible promise of tomorrow will nevertheless come.

So faith does not come from the physical, the material, the measurable or the quantifiable. It is not determined by what we can see, smell, hear, taste and touch. Rather, faith depends on an inner knowing and a real hope for what is not yet—a knowing and a hope that originates not from some imagination of our minds, but from the assurance that comes only from God.

Without confidence, we have no hope—only wishful thinking. Without hope, we have no faith—only fantasy. Be convicted in your heart and mind today of the reality that is yet to be, and boldly persevere toward that unseeable end. Yeshua is coming, and God is continually keeping His promises—believe, and do not draw back, but hold on to the hope of your soul...

PRAYER

O Father, why are faith and hope so hard? Increase my faith, Master, by reminding me of Your truth, and then embolden my soul to believe and hope with confidence and conviction. Help me to not mistake wishfulness for faith, but rather teach me to see without seeing, and to believe without receiving. I praise You, ADONAI, for Your everlasting promises; only upon You may I always and faithfully hope...

BE NOT CARRIED AWAY

> יֵשׁוּעַ, Yeshua *the* Messiah *is* the same yesterday, and today, and to the ages; be not carried away by various and strange teachings. –עִבְרִים Iv'riym 13:8-9a

Are you being carried away by strange teachings? Are you believing things that simply aren't true? For instance, you probably think that the statement, "Yeshua is the same yesterday, today and forever," is an assertion of His eternal existence. No doubt, in the beginning was the Word, the Word was with God, and the Word was God. Indeed, He who became flesh and lived among us is, in fact, eternal…

…but that has barely anything at all to do with this verse.

It's ironic, actually, that this particular verse would so often be isolated and taken out of context, given that the passage is actually a warning about *false teachings*. What the verse is *really* asserting is that despite "various and strange teachings" (like those that call Yeshua's salvation, sacrifice, and second coming into question; or cause people to be distracted over relatively inconsequential things such as eating; or lead them into doubt about the future and cause them to fall away), the truth of Yeshua the Messiah will never change. That is, He is "the same yesterday" when we first learned of Him, "today" as we are still being exhorted to believe, "and to the ages" as we persevere in hope and faith. Yes, the eternal nature of the Word is naturally embedded in this truth—but that is not the author's point.

Drawing a wrong (or, at least, incomplete) and superficial conclusion about Yeshua is indicative of the problem we tend to have with embracing the warning against false teachings.

While a little effort, context and logic goes a long way to grasping the simple teachings of Scripture, many of us prefer to just absorb what others have put in the work to learn—or contrive. This leaves us each vulnerable to the creative—and sometimes manipulative—minds of men, causing us to concoct "various and strange" Yeshuas that only somewhat resemble the real One.

So now the question remains: if we can be taught by teachers to misunderstand and misapply such a simple text, how much more susceptible are we to "being carried away by various and strange teachings"—the conclusions of which are far more threatening to our faith? Have we put ourselves in danger by trusting certain teachers, while failing to thoroughly verify the things that they say?

Be careful about who and what you listen to, simply accepting and repeating teachings you have heard. Indeed, you might already believe more "various and strange teachings" than you know...

PRAYER

Yeshua, I praise You, for in You dwells the fullness of the Deity, who has existed forever! Send Your Ruach, Master, that I may know and understand Your Scriptures, and not be carried away by various and strange teachings—simply affirming and repeating what I have heard. Help me, God, to keep my eyes fixed on Yeshua, the author and perfecter of faith. Thank You, ADONAI, for giving me a mind and a ruach, that I may read and grasp the truth of Your perfect word...

HAVING SEEN THEIR FAITH

> And יֵשׁוּעַ, Yeshua, having seen their faith, said
> to the paralytic, "Child, your sins are forgiven."
> –MARK 2:5

One time in K'far-Nachum, Yeshua was speaking the word
to a house so full of people that there was not a single bit of
room left—not even at the door. So when four men arrived,
determined for their paralytic friend to see the Master, they
climbed on the roof, broke it up, and lowered the man on his
mat through the opening. Surely the homeowner must have
been greatly alarmed at the sudden uncovering of his roof!
But what the Master saw being uncovered was something
entirely different—something of far greater, eternal value.

What some might have seen as an act of desperate destruction, Yeshua saw as an act of pure faith. The faith of these four
men could literally be *seen* in the actions they took to close the
distance between their sick friend and his Healer. But more
than that, it was the faith of the four men—not any faith of
the paralytic himself—that led to the paralytic's forgiveness
and eventual healing. Yeshua had seen *their* faith deployed on
their friend's behalf—and clearly, it was more than enough.

When we truly have faith, there may be every rational reason
not to act on it. But while the deed might appear unreasonable
or misguided to others, the actions that flow from true faith
are nearly impossible to resist. This does not give us license to
act foolishly, hoping to fulfill what is only wishful thinking.
Rather, true faith should cause us to act outwardly—even
unexpectedly—because we ourselves have seen in advance
with the fearlessness of Messiah.

Our internal faith can not only be seen and put into action for ourselves, it can be extended to others and acted upon on their behalf. Indeed, such action may create an opportunity to prove faith's unreasonable reality to all who encounter it. When others are weak in body or spirit, we can enact our faith by figuratively *and sometimes literally* picking them up, and laying them at the Master's feet.

When you see a friend in need, don't just pray for their faith to increase—put yours into action! How visible is your faith today? What kind of faith can the Master see in you?

PRAYER

Master Yeshua, increase my faith, so that I may be big and bold in my actions. Help me to not hoard my faith inwardly for myself, but to enact it outwardly on behalf of others without fear. Thank You, ADONAI, for not limiting the great things I can believe for and do in You. Teach me, Abba, to have an outrageous faith that exceeds my understanding; show me the way to break through and uncover my faith in You…

YOUR FAITH HAS SAVED YOU

> And He was looking around to see her who did this; and the woman, having been afraid and trembling, and knowing what was done to her, came and fell down before Him and told Him all the truth. And He said to her, "Daughter, your faith has saved you; go away in peace, and be whole from your affliction." –MARK 5:32-34

She had been chronically bleeding for twelve years. Though she spent all she had on doctors, not only did they not make her any better, but she eventually got worse. Then one day, she heard about Yeshua and immediately knew what she had to do. Pushing her way through the crowd, she managed to just barely touch His outer garment, and instantly, the bleeding stopped—she knew in her body that she had been healed. At that same moment, the Master became aware that power had gone out of Him, and He turned to see her... trembling. Knowing what was done to her, she fell down before Him, and the Master pronounced her salvation.

Whether we or a loved one are suffering from an acute or chronic illness, we will often cry out to Yeshua for His healing touch. We believe that healing can come in an instant—that if He will only reach out across whatever expanse that separates us, His divine contact will bring about immediate change. So we pray and we hope that He would be moved, and we would soon receive His special touch. And yet, in this case, it was the *woman* touching *Yeshua*—indeed, merely His outer garment—that brought about her supernatural healing.

We spiritualize "Yeshua's touch" into something more meta-physical, believing He can heal us from afar—and He certainly can. But the kind of healing this woman received was not in any way distant or removed by time or space. On the contrary, it involved *her* literally touching *Him*—actually being in physical contact with the Messiah Himself. How, then, do we receive such healing today, when the Master is not physically right there in front of us for us to reach out and grab hold of?

Knowing that one day we too would need this kind of healing, maybe Yeshua has already provided the answer. "Daughter, your faith has saved you; go away in peace, and be whole from your affliction." By telling the woman that it was her *faith* that saved her, perhaps the Master was also telling us that we can still touch His *power* even when we are physically unable to touch *Him*. How much of her healing came by touch, and how much of it came by faith? Perhaps all we need to do, in our desperation and hope, is to simply reach out in faith *and believe...*

PRAYER

Master Yeshua, I confess to You now: when I remain unhealed it breeds doubt in my heart—please help my unbelief! My Savior, I know You can touch me from wherever You are, but help me to believe that I can still touch Your power, even when You're not physically here. Increase my faith, ADONAI, and make me whole; restore me from my suffering and affliction. Help me to enact my faith, O Mighty God, and trust in Your unlimited power to save.

HE WAS NOT ABLE

> And יֵשׁוּעַ, Yeshua said to them, "A prophet is not
> without honor, except in his own homeland, and
> among his relatives, and in his own house"; and He
> was not able to do any powerful act there, except,
> having put hands on a few infirmed people, He
> healed THEM. And He was in wonder because of
> their unbelief. –MARK 6:4-6

Having traveled the Land for some time, teaching and doing powerful acts among the people, at one point the Master
returned home. He needed no introduction there, as everyone
knew Him, yet He was met with astonishment and skepticism
as He taught in the synagogue. Hearing His wisdom, and
learning of the mighty things He had done, the people "were
being stumbled at Him" (6:3): how could little Yeshua, whom
we have known since infancy—whose mother and brothers
and sisters are our neighbors—be capable of all this... much
less be the Messiah!

And this left the Master in wonder and disbelief. How could
the people who had known Him longer and better than
anyone be so cold and unreceptive? How could they be so un-
convinced? It was because they were too *familiar* with Him...
too informal—indeed, "a prophet is not without honor, except
in his own homeland." And so, incredibly, the Master Yeshua was rendered inoperative, unable to do any powerful act
among His family and oldest friends.

Why do so many of us, as believers in Yeshua, not do and see
powerful acts as He said we would? Why is Yeshua's power
not mightily manifesting among us? Perhaps it is because we

lack the belief, and are skeptical that such power is accessible and real. Or perhaps it is because we are too familiar—too informal—with Yeshua. Too often, we count Him as our companion, copilot and confidant, and not often enough our God, Master and King.

Has your friendship with God lost its sense of awe? Has the intimacy you seek with Him robbed Him of your reverence? Be sure to give Yeshua all the honor He is due—otherwise, you too may prevent Him from doing His powerful acts in you...

PRAYER

Master Yeshua, forgive me for being too familiar with You—for treating You as a sidekick instead of as my Savior. Too often I have taken You for granted, either forgetting You are there, or using You merely as a receptacle for my emotions and complaints. I praise You, Yeshua, for You are worthy of all the honor due Your Name. Receive my praise and glory, O God, and do a powerful act in me.

TO THIS GENERATION

> And having sighed deeply in His רוּחַ, ruach, He said, "Why does this generation seek after a sign? אָמֵן, Amen, I say to you: no sign will be given to this generation." –MARK 8:12

Reports of the Master had spread throughout the Land, causing great consternation for the religious authorities. When He arrived in Dalmanutha with His disciples, the P'rushiym were quick to confront Him, "disput[ing] with Him, looking for a sign from Him from the Heaven, tempting Him" (8:11). The fact that any of His own people would reject Him—especially those who ought to have known better—weighed heavily on the Master's heart. "And having sighed deeply in His רוּחַ, ruach, He said, 'Why does this generation seek after a sign? אָמֵן, Amen, I say to you: no sign will be given to this generation.'"

Their multifold motivations aside, the antagonism from the P'rushiym was blatant. By essentially demanding proof from Yeshua that He was indeed the Messiah, it was not so much aimed at ascertaining the truth as it was an attempt to undermine and injure His message. The truth was, in a real way, irrelevant to their agenda. Any proof He offered would simply be dismissed and explained away. The Master, having none of it, would not offer them fodder for their backhanded schemes. A generation which sought a sign that it would not believe would not be receiving one from Him.

In every generation there are those who demand proof from God despite having no intention of being persuaded should any evidence be provided. The demand is insincere; the antagonism, palpably authentic. What, then, will God do with a generation of "believers" who do the same? ...those who claim with their mouths that they believe, yet deny the truth through their actions—and their inaction? What signs should we expect to see from God—what indications of rescue from our shrinking bubble of safety and freedom—when we are the ones who sat idly by, retreated, risked little, and stopped trying to make Yeshua known to a degenerate generation?

Just as in Yeshua's day, our empty, signless generation nevertheless has access to God's continuing testimony. We must repent for our inaction and rise up to meet our day's hopelessness with the unflinching hope of His word and a persistent faith in the Messiah Yeshua. If our faith is true, we ought to need no sign or miraculous intervention to trust in His hand and have confidence in His unending promises—even when He does not appear to be answering our calls. Either God is equally real in good times as in bad, or He is not real at all.

Let your actions match your rhetoric; stake your life on what you claim to believe. "No sign will be given to this generation," because God wants *you* to be the proof that people need.

PRAYER

ADONAI, I praise Your Name; forgive me for my insincerity while I have demanded Your compliance. Convict my heart of Your watchfulness and patience, O God, for I have dismissed and undermined You in my inaction, if not my words. Wake me up, Master, that I may not merely wrap myself in the comfort of an echo chamber of self-righteous opinions. Let this generation not seek a sign, but You, Wonderful One—and let it see You, and find You, in me.

TELL NO ONE

> And יֵשׁוּעַ, Yeshua and His disciples went out to the villages of Cæsarea Philippi, and on the way He was questioning His disciples, saying to them, "Who do men say Me to be?" And they told Him, saying, "*Some say You are* יוֹחָנָן, Yochanan the Immerser, and others אֵלִיָּהוּ, Eliyahu, but others *say You are* one of the prophets." And He was questioning them, "And you—who do you say Me to be?" כֵּיפָא, Keifa, answering, said to Him, "You are the Messiah." And He sternly warned them that they should tell no one about it…. –MARK 8:27-30

One day, the Master asked His disciples, "Who do you say Me to be?" Keifa replied, "You are the Messiah." The Master then "sternly warned them that they should tell no one about it," presumably because He did not want premature, widespread revelation of who He was to impede His work. Yeshua would eventually go on to endure suffering, rejection and death exactly as He said, and then rise on the third day in victorious completion of His divinely-appointed mission.

Who, then, were the disciples no longer supposed to tell? Who still needed to be shielded from the truth? Whatever reason the Master had for wanting to maintain a level of anonymity, surely everything was now sufficiently exposed. It would have made no sense for the disciples to continue keeping the Master's temporary secret once He had been fully revealed.

So why is it that, of all the Master's commands, the order to "tell no one" may be the one we most consistently keep today?

Whereas the Master wanted no one to know He was the Messiah for the sake of the work, we "tell no one" because the opportunity doesn't present itself, or we don't want to push our beliefs on others, or we're uncomfortable, or afraid, or some other such excuse. We keep the truth to ourselves because our silence serves our interests. When the disciples told no one, it was so that the work would not be hindered. When we tell no one, we hinder the very work now complete in the Master.

Yeshua's instruction to His disciples to "tell no one" He was the Messiah was never intended to be carried out forever. He issued that order strictly as a short-lived, strategic effort toward the conclusion of His work. Stop perfectly fulfilling a command that Yeshua never meant for you to keep. Open your mouth, and be filled with the boldness of the Ruach HaQodesh! For Yeshua is the Messiah, and today He is sternly warning us that we must tell *everyone* about it...

PRAYER

Father, I praise You for the salvation of Your Son! Teach my heart and mind that the time to tell everyone about Yeshua is always *now*. Help me, God, to not be afraid, ashamed or self-absorbed, such that I fail to share Yeshua's hope and salvation everywhere I go. I glorify Your Name, ADONAI; open my mouth, that I may reveal Your secret to the world. Make me bold, wise and discerning, Master, that my hindrance of Your work would forever end today.

BE HELPING MY UNBELIEF

> [The child's father said,] "But if You are able to do anything, help us, having compassion on us!" And יֵשׁוּעַ, Yeshua said to him, "If you are able! all things are possible to the one that is believing." Immediately the father of the child, having cried out, said, "I believe! Be helping my unbelief." –MARK 9:22-24

There is a little voice inside your head that's always speaking. Sometimes it's difficult to make out; other times, it rages. No matter how much you exercise your faith, that little voice of unbelief is always there, trying to undermine and derail you. It gnaws on your thoughts, hoping to expose something sensitive and raw. Its goal is to eventually drown out your faith—to subdue and replace it—so that unbelief rules your heart even when your head knows better.

The Master teaches us that "all things are possible to the one that is believing," yet from the moment we hear this, we doubt it to be true. For how many things have we believed, yet not seen their fulfillment? For how long have we cried out and waited for a rescue that has yet to arrive? In the face of the call for faith, our experience screams otherwise as the voice of unbelief reminds us of all the things we've prayed for— believed God for—that have never come to pass.

But the Master says that all things are possible not simply if we believe, but also "if you are able!" By enabling the voice of unbelief, we disable our ability to believe. To believe God for all things depends upon our capacity to push aside and forget the many times we have perceived our prayers as unanswered— to silence the doubt based on those experiences—and then to remember that despite *our* inabilities, *Yeshua* is able in all things, no matter what we've seen or how long we've waited.

We make our belief shallow and ineffective, then, when we ignore the existence of the nagging voice of unbelief. It will never keep quiet—it will persist in any way it can—so to pretend it isn't there only makes us susceptible to its whispers. Instead, let us first acknowledge that voice, and then ask Yeshua for help to quash it, so that we may be able to fully believe again without limits.

What are you believing—and doubting—for today? Acknowledge your unbelief, then silence it, and hear only the voice of faith.

PRAYER

Abba, Father, as faith and doubt wrestle within me, make me able to believe again that all things are possible. Teach me, God, to reconcile my faith against the background noise of unbelief, and to learn how to hear only Your perfect voice above the din. I praise You, Yeshua, for even in my unbelief, You are always able—You are never failing—no matter what I may perceive to the contrary. Thank You, ADONAI, for hearing my prayer and knowing my need. I believe, my Master! Be helping my unbelief...

FOR THE STIFFNESS
OF YOUR HEART

> And the פְּרוּשִׁים, P'rushiym, having come near, ques-
> tioned Him, *asking* if it is permitted for a husband
> to send away a wife (*they were* tempting Him).
> And He, answering, said to them, "What did מֹשֶׁה,
> Mosheh command you?" And they said, "מֹשֶׁה, Mo-
> sheh allowed *a man* to WRITE A DOCUMENT
> OF DIVORCE, AND TO SEND *HER* AWAY."
> And יֵשׁוּעַ, Yeshua said to them, "He wrote you
> this command for the stiffness of your heart...."
> –MARK 10:2-5

When the P'rushiym tried to trip up Yeshua with a question about divorce (although divorce is not the point of this
devotional!), the Master taught them a thing or two—about
themselves. Yes, Mosheh had permitted divorce, but, as the
Master tells us, that is not the way it was "from the beginning" (10:6). On the contrary, "what God joined together, let
not man separate" (10:9); divorce was never part of the plan.

So if God did not envision divorce, the first question that
comes to mind is: why did Mosheh permit it? Why would
Mosheh—presumably with God's consent—allow what was
obviously illicit? Yeshua reveals the startling truth: "He wrote
you this command for the stiffness of your heart." Though God
hates divorce (Malachi 2:16), and this was not His way from
the beginning, Mosheh permitted it because of the stiffness
in people's hearts. The Father acquiesced to the stubbornness
of His children.

That, then, leads to the second question: why would God allow the violation of His created order just to accommodate our stubbornness? Does He do it in the hopes that we won't go through with our hard-hearted plans? Or is He perhaps taking a softer approach so that we will not break away from Him so far as to become permanently broken? Whatever His reason, even if He makes allowance for an obstinate heart—even if He gives an inch for our rotten core to have its way—we need to ask ourselves if that is really the way we want to go. Even if we can find daylight between the black and white of any of God's commands—enough space to operate "lawfully" in the gray—is that really the place we want to live for Messiah?

There is a difference—a huge difference—between what we're allowed to do and what we ought. Just because we are *technically* permitted to behave a certain way doesn't make it in any way good or right or pleasing in the eyes of the Father. What is God allowing you to get away with today, even though He hates it? Maybe it's time to reevaluate your opinions and motivations, and take a good long look at the stiffness of your heart...

PRAYER

I bless You, Father, for Your mercy and love. Thank You for seeing and knowing my heart—both in softness and in stiffness. Please forgive me, ADONAI, for trying to find loopholes and shortcuts in Your word that allow me to weasel my way around Your perfect will. Bend me, Master—break me if You must—but cause me to fall in line with all that is truly right. Let me not accept any concessions for my stubbornness, O God, but teach me to walk only in full compliance with Your heart...

FORGIVE

> "And whenever you stand praying, if you have any-
> thing against anyone, forgive, so that your Father
> who is in the Heavens will also forgive you your
> missteps." –MARK 11:25

Perhaps you've mostly forgotten—pushed it into the background, locked it away somewhere, hoping it will never again
see the light of day. Or maybe you put it away on purpose
because you like keeping it close by—knowing that you
shouldn't, but refusing to give it up—so you can take it out
from time to time to play around with and enjoy. Nevertheless, it's still there—possibly lying dormant, possibly festering
over. But either way, it's neither being thrown away, nor dealt
with.

Unforgiveness is one of those things that tends to keep coming back to mess with you in unexpected and unhealthy ways.
It seeps out from the place you try to cage it, tainting all it
touches: your hopes, your state of mind, and—perhaps worst
of all—your relationships with others. It won't go away—it
can't go away—until you finally come to grips with it. You
may feel like it's gone at this moment, but eventually it's effects will be felt, and you will find it exactly where you left
it—grotesque and very much alive.

Yeshua teaches us that our unforgiveness hinders God from
forgiving us. Since unforgiveness is apparently a wall that we
ourselves erect, God, therefore, is unwilling to climb over it
or knock it down. When we pray, we must not be holding
anything against anyone for something they did (or something
we *think* they did). Rather, if we are harboring unforgiveness,

Yeshua says *we* must forgive, so that the *Father* will also forgive. We are responsible for—and capable of—taking out that trash, and removing that barrier once and for all.

When we ask God to forgive us for what we've done, He is first going to want to know if we have done for others what we are asking Him to do for us. Only a heart that is willing to forgive is capable of fully receiving forgiveness. If you don't let go of the past, the Father can't help you going forward. As hard as it may be, you need to unlock the monster of unforgiveness and set it free. Today is the day to truly forgive...

...and, finally, to forget.

PRAYER

Father, as I search my heart today for the things I am holding against others, please help me to let go of past hurts—or perceived offenses—and to truly and finally forgive. Teach me to once and for all unload this poisonous burden and to be released into the freedom of forgiveness. I praise You, Abba, for healing me of my past, and for forgiving me of my own missteps against You. Thank You, Master, for my brand new, unburdened, future. Today I am free—and forgiven—in You.

THE SCRIPTURES AND
THE POWER OF GOD

> And the צְדוּקִים, Tzaduqiym, who say there is not a
> Rising Again, came to Him; and they were ques-
> tioning Him, saying.... *"Now* there were seven
> brothers, and the first took a wife, but dying, he
> left no seed; and the second took her, [and so on.
> In] the Rising Again, whenever they *all* rise, of
> which of them will she be *the* wife (for *each of*
> the seven had her as *a* wife)?" יֵשׁוּעַ, Yeshua said to
> them, "Do you not go astray because of this, not
> knowing the Scriptures, nor the power of God?"
> –MARK 12:18,20-24

We're pretty brilliant aren't we? We humans can come up
with such amazing stuff that it makes one wonder if we were
ever really mortal in the first place. Surely our reasoning is
so sublime that we can dispute not only rational thought,
but biology, reality, sound logic, and God Himself. We can
fathom the mysteries of the universe with no concern that we
could possibly be wrong. Indeed, who is god but us? And who
is a rock, except ourselves?

The Tzaduqiym had come to Yeshua not with a legitimate
question or an inquiring mind. Rather, their intention was to
assert what they believed to be true, and then challenge Yeshua
to refute it. It didn't matter that their premise was faulty or
their argument hypothetical. Honest debate or the discovery
of truth was never the goal. They knew they had devised the
perfect puzzle to stump the Messiah and prove their point.

That was the sole purpose of what they set out to do... and failed miserably.

For those of us who are so audacious as to go up against and question the wisdom and reality of God, the Master has a question for us in return: "Do you not go astray because of this, not knowing the Scriptures, nor the power of God?" There is no wisdom, no knowledge, no logic, and no reality that is above, beyond, greater than or equal to the Scriptures or God's infinite power. No evidence can disprove it; no reasoning can refute it—yet our arrogance can obscure it and keep us from knowing the truth.

Without the pure light of God's perfect word, we are nothing but blind wanderers feeling around in the dark. The truth of God's reality is all around us, and no matter how sightless or stupid we are, we will inevitably bump into or brush up against it. But we will only ever go astray as long as we fail to know God's power and His Scriptures—the word of God that testifies to and reveals that awesome power.

Do you not go astray, not knowing the Scriptures? Set aside your own arrogant ideas, or else you'll never know.

PRAYER

ADONAI my God, Your word is perfect, and Your power is to be praised! As I open Your Book, Abba, please open my heart and reveal to my mind even an inch of the depth of Your wisdom and truth. Crush my arrogance, God, and confound my knowledge, that I will stop thinking so highly of my own thoughts, opinions and point of view. Teach me, Master, to see the reality of Your righteousness, and to bow my conceited, human reasoning to Your loving and perfect will...

DRAW ME TO YOUR REIGN

> [The Scribe said,] "Teacher, in truth you have spoken well that He is one, AND THERE IS NONE OTHER BUT HE; and to LOVE HIM OUT OF ALL THE HEART, and out of all the understanding, AND OUT OF ALL THE STRENGTH, and to love one's neighbor as one's self is more than all the whole burnt-offerings and sacrifices." And יֵשׁוּעַ, Yeshua, having seen him, that he answered with understanding, said to him, "You are not far from the Reign of God...." –MARK 12:32-34A

The religious leaders had come to start a dispute with the Master. Surely, He was a fraud. But when Yeshua answered them well, one Scribe—perhaps curious, perhaps surprised—felt led to question Him further. When the Master replied, the Scribe found himself in agreement, and affirmed that Yeshua had spoken the truth. But the exchange seemed to take everyone aback when Yeshua affirmed the Scribe's response in return, stating that he was already close to the kingdom of God. The Scribe had been prepared through his understanding of the Scriptures.

For this one Scribe, his knowledge and understanding of the Scriptures drew him near to the Reign. He had learned and studied the word in truth, and when it came time to meet the Master, he was already close. He then needed only to believe that Yeshua is the Messiah to go the rest of the way.

The question is: does it also work the other way around?

For those of us already believing in Yeshua, how close are we really to the Reign of God? Could a belief in Yeshua not grounded in a knowledge and understanding of God's word actually be insufficient for entering God's kingdom? Is it possible to even know the authentic Messiah without knowing what the Scriptures say? In the case of the Scribe, Yeshua judged him not on whether he believed He was the Messiah, but on his understanding of a truth that challenged his religious convictions. So for those of us who already believe, will our closeness to God's Reign also be judged by that same standard?

Without a doubt, no one can enter God's kingdom unless he comes in through the Messiah Yeshua. But no matter where we jump into the cycle of belief and understanding—either by first believing in Yeshua, or by first knowing God's word—our journey will be abruptly halted if we do not have a solid and truthful understanding of the Scriptures. It's not enough to have an idea of God and the Messiah if it's not built on the foundation of His word. A Messiah of our own mind and making cannot save.

Would the Master see *you* answering Him with understanding today? How close would He deem *you* to be to the Reign of God?

PRAYER

Master Yeshua, I praise Your Name, Your wisdom, and Your truth; give me the understanding that comes only from Your word. Let me not be led astray, God, believing that I am prepared to enter the Reign without the fullest knowledge and understanding of Your word I am able to gain. Make me unsatisfied, Father, with the religion of man, that I may hunger only for Your word of truth. See me, ADONAI, and judge me true; draw me close and into Your Reign.

THE END IS NOT YET

> "And when you hear of wars and reports of wars, be not troubled; these need to be, but the end *is* not yet..." –MARK 13:7

Every generation suspects it may be the last—some with better reason than others—believing that the state of the world is the worst it's ever been. When we are young, we tend to see things in one dimension, sometimes fatalistically and often unnuanced. Then as we age, we judge today against the backdrop of our yesterdays—and, many times, yesterday can seem a great deal safer than tomorrow.

As difficult as it is to imagine—especially these days—we won't know in advance how bad things will really be right before the end. Perhaps it is even beyond what we can fathom. What type of warfare will we ultimately bear? Which self-destructive (and society-destructive) ideas will have taken root in younger minds? Indeed, how much worse can it get, given that each generation has a knack for taking its perversion and devastation another step further than the one before. Only the undoing of whole societies has previously been able to reset our collective sanity even to a degree. Yet the carnage of the end will eventually encompass the entire world, and only a select few will have any idea what is happening.

So while we work and wait for the end—for the Master Yeshua's glorious and victorious return—He wants us, first of all, to not be disturbed by all the madness and incomprehensible behavior we see. Though not oblivious to it, He mainly wants us focused on Him, not on how terrible or hopeless things appear to be. He wants us to keep our wits about us, and to watch out for false teachers, false prophets and false messiahs, who would take advantage and lead us to our own destruction. He wants us praying and remaining steadfast in the faith; He wants us concentrating our actions on the dissemination of His hope and His word.

So when you hear of wars and reports of wars—when you observe havoc, intimidation and violence; when you sense the rise of socialism, communism and revisionism; when you see the signs of economic, linguistic and biological revolution and anarchy—fix your eyes on Yeshua, and be not troubled. Take heart, stay strong, stand firm in the faith, and fear not those who can kill the body, but not the soul. The Master is exhorting us today to persevere and endure in Him—that though all these things still need to be... "the end *is* not yet..."

PRAYER

O Yeshua, it is growing hard to bear... I eagerly await Your triumphant return! Have mercy on Your people, O God, and shorten the days of evil for the sake of Your chosen. As the end draws near, Master, encourage my heart; help me to stand firm and to never lose hope for my salvation. Guard my mind, Father, that I may not be led astray in fear, and overcome my troubled thoughts, that I will find peace—and victory—in You...

STAY AWAKE!

> "Watch out; *keep* alert; for you have not known when the time is…. *Stay* awake, therefore, for you have not known when the master of the house will come: either at evening, or at midnight, or at *the* rooster-crowing, or at the morning; so that, having come suddenly, he may not find you sleeping. And what I say to you, I say to all: *stay* awake!"
>
> −MARK 13:33, 35-37

As the days drone on and life remains a blur, we lose momentum and purpose for the future. Caught up in the monotony, we misinterpret activity as progress, and each day slips seamlessly into the next. Whatever time and energy we might have left over for our walk with God inevitably fails to escape the same sluggishness. Though both the Reign and the end are near but not yet, we are falling asleep, being anesthetized by technology, convenience, the endless pursuit of comfort, and the perpetual cycle of busyness.

Yet such exercise in numbness is incompatible with our heavenly call. Rather than settling down with the soothing repetition of daily existence, we are meant to be actively engaged with the life of Messiah—wrestling with a world that would rather be sleeping than be saved. But as long as we as a Body remain largely bloated and immobile, finding excuses for not advancing the cause of Messiah—or imagining that we are when we're really not—we will continue to slumber through the Day when it eventually comes, and will ultimately miss the arrival of our Master.

We must not be caught napping when Yeshua returns for His Chosen. Rather, the Master expects to find us hard at work, laboring without ceasing in the fields of the harvest, with one eye looking expectantly toward the heavens. Though the signs of the times always signal His imminent return, He nevertheless warns us to not grow weary in the waiting, but to be ever-vigilant.

We must, therefore, "watch out" for that which will lengthen and deepen our slumber.

We must "*keep* alert," for we "have not known when the time is."

And we must "*stay* awake," for we "have not known when the master of the house will come."

Be invigorated, "so that, having come suddenly, he may not find you sleeping," only to awaken and find that He has already gone. Arise, followers of Messiah! Wake up, chosen ones! Do not grow tired in doing right and working in all ways and all things only for the Master. "And what I say to you, I say to all: *stay* awake!"

PRAYER

Come quickly, Master Yeshua, and find me not sleeping soundly, but wide awake—walking with You, and at work! Let me not slumber through life and stumble in my walk, as I gradually forget that You still intend to come. Teach me, ADONAI, to watch out, remembering Your eternal purpose for me in every waking moment. Prepare me for Your return, O Son of God, that I may be ready for Your arrival. Revive me, keep me alert, and help me to remain awake for You...

ARE YOU THE MESSIAH?

> But He was keeping silent, and did not answer anything. Again the כֹּהֵן הַגָּדוֹל, Kohen HaGadol was questioning Him, and said to Him, "Are you the Messiah—the Son of the Blessed *One?*" And יֵשׁוּעַ, Yeshua said, "I am." –MARK 14:61-62A

Following a steady stream of false witnesses, it seemed that all the Master had to do was remain silent, and His sham of a trial would soon come to end. As the Kohen HaGadol began to badger Yeshua, he finally asked Him directly, "Are you the Messiah—the Son of the Blessed *One?*" What happened next must have left the Ko'haniym and Sanhedrin in jaw-dropping disbelief. Though He appeared to be mere moments from release, the Master nevertheless opened His mouth and testified in the affirmative, "I am." Regaining his composure, the Kohen then tore his garments and declared, "What need have we of further witnesses?" (14:63).

When the Master was finally called as His own witness, it appeared the only thing standing between Him and freedom was whether or not He would choose to *lie.* Perhaps if He had denied the matter, He might have escaped the agony awaiting Him, and gone on to live a peaceful, insignificant life. Yet the Master entertained no such thought, instead refusing to renounce the truth, and knowingly sealing His fate. No false testimony was needed—the truth was sufficient to establish guilt in the eyes of His persecutors.

In a day such as ours when words no longer hold their meaning, and truth is whatever people want it to be, our words—true or not—will ultimately be irrelevant to any persecutor.

As it was with the Master, our captors and oppressors will do anything they can to justify their fear, hatred, and fight for dominance. If we claim the Name of Yeshua, that will be enough justification for them. Neither our rational explanation nor any desperate excuse will save us from our fate.

When standing in judgment before men—for any reason— we may try to help our cause by denying the truth. But one day, when we are standing in judgment before God, we will have to answer for how we defend ourselves. For Yeshua, truth was ever the only choice. Though lying (blatantly or through omission) may seem prudent at the time, we must not let fear of what may happen to us be our motivator. Even when we would like to avoid negative consequences—and especially when we are being persecuted in Yeshua's Name— as Messiah-followers, our only choice is to always and at all times speak the truth…

…for only the truth can truly set us free…

PRAYER

Father, strengthen my resolve, that I may always and at all times speak the truth. Help me to overcome the feelings that lead me to hide or obscure the truth—even to outright lie— just to protect myself. Convict my heart, Master, so that my trust in You will always exceed my fear. Make me a reliable witness, ADONAI, that I may never be silent, but boldly testify to the truth of Your blessed and holy Name.

THE INSCRIPTION
OF HIS ACCUSATION

> And it was the third hour, and they crucified Him, and the inscription of His accusation was written above—"The King of the Jews." –MARK 15:25-26

All the people were mocking Him and speaking evil: the Roman soldiers, those passing by, the chief Ko'haniym, the Sof'riym, even those being crucified beside Him. For some, the mockery came out of a place of vindictiveness; for others, from a sense of betrayal. Many had dared Him to be—and others had hoped that He was—the Messiah, the long-awaited King of the Jews. Seeing Him there now, mangled, crucified and condemned, it seemed maybe they were justified—or, perhaps, just simply wrong.

Sentenced as a criminal, the accusation of His so-called crime was inscribed upon His execution stake: "The King of the Jews." Thanks to the Roman governor, the charge did not include *claims* to kingship, nor even *false* claims. The Master's "crime," then—not only in the eyes of Rome, but in the hearts of many in Israel—was that He was, indeed, King. And so the people who had once asked God for a king rejected the King of kings when He finally arrived.

We ask God for help, for relief, for deliverance—but what if the way He helps and delivers us doesn't meet with our approval or expectations? What if our rescue comes with conditions, like personal responsibility, abandoning worldly gratifications, and the requirement to change the way we think and behave? Would we too find such salvation repulsive and worthy of our contempt? Would we too reject and mock and deny and punish our one, true King?

Yeshua met no one's expectations, but instead surpassed them all, coming as a Messianic King whom no one had envisioned or anticipated. The King of kings does battle not for earthly dominions, but for our very souls. He takes possession not of our lands and resources, but of the entirety of our lives. Don't expect Yeshua to be whoever you want Him to be or wish that He were. Only expect Him to be exactly who you need, and to continually commit the high "crime" of being King...

PRAYER

King Yeshua, I submit myself to Your awesome and eternal authority; do with me as You will. Help me, Master, to place no expectations of my own making upon You, but only to expect You to care for me as You deem fit for Your loyal subject. Teach my heart, Father, to accept the rule of Your Son over my whole life, that I will never resist or reject His commands. Forgive me, ADONAI, for retaining rulership over myself... I now relinquish all control and authority to You.

BELIEVE THE UNBELIEVABLE

And יֵשׁוּעַ, Yeshua, having let go a loud sound, breathed His last. And the curtain of the Temple was split in two, from top to bottom; and the centurion who was standing opposite Him, having seen the way that He breathed His last, said, "Truly this man was *the* Son of God." –Mark 15:37-39

Mocked, beaten and humiliated, the time had come for Israel's king to be killed. Crucified on His execution stake, the Master endured that tortuous punishment as an innocent lamb led to slaughter. Suddenly, the whole land became covered in darkness, and the Master cried out to God, letting go a loud sound, and then breathed His last. The earth shook, the rocks were split, and the thick, huge curtain of the Temple—from top to bottom—was torn in two. Truly, it was awesome.

A crowd of onlookers surrounded Yeshua, watching—some in horror, some in glee—as the Messiah took His final breath. Yet no one could have anticipated what would happen next. A Roman centurion stood opposite Yeshua with an up-close and personal view of the whole thing. After witnessing the breathtaking display, he stood there—astonished at this criminal Jew—and then, in complete amazement, opened his mouth and declared the truth: "Truly this man was *the* Son of God." A mind changed in an afternoon.

The spectacle of Yeshua's death was clearly awe-inspiring—enough to move an unbeliever to confess the unbelievable. But if the manner of the Master's death was this impressive, how much more impressed ought one to be with the revelation of His resurrection—the most astounding feat of all? And yet, while many witnessed the Master's sensational death, no one saw His rising again. He appeared after the fact, alive and well—the only witness: an empty tomb.

It takes no amount of faith to believe your eyes; it requires all the faith in the world to believe what you've only been told. Our amazement should not merely be in Yeshua's death and resurrection, but in the conviction of our hearts and minds that every bit of it is true.

If you believe today that Yeshua died and rose again, then you can also believe Him for even more that you have yet to see. Don't wait to see it before you believe it—but have faith for the unbelievable...

PRAYER

Master Yeshua, You are utterly astonishing and amazing, and I praise Your great and awesome Name! I believe with my whole heart in Your death and resurrection, though I never witnessed either one with my very own eyes. Help me, Father, to now believe for things in my own life that have yet to be— and that seem almost as impossible as the way You gave Your Son for me. Teach me, God, to not wait to believe until I see, but to trust fully in You. Grow my faith, increase my trust, and remind me to believe the unbelievable.

SPEECHLESS

> And the Messenger, answering [Z'khar'yah], said to him, "I am נַבְרִיאֵל, Gav'riyel, who has been standing near in the presence of God, and I was sent to speak to you, and to proclaim this Good News to you. And look! you will be silent and not able to speak until the day that these things come to pass, because you did not believe my words, which will be fulfilled in their season." –LUKE 1:19-20

Z'khar'yah was righteous before God, a kohen in active service. He and his wife were both advanced in their days, and though they were "going on blamelessly in all the commands and righteousnesses of ADONAI" (1:6), she was nevertheless barren. When a Messenger of ADONAI appeared to Z'khar'-yah, declaring that their prayers for a child would soon be answered, his initial reaction quickly grew to disbelief, and He questioned the Messenger's pronouncement. The Messenger responded by striking Z'khar'yah speechless "because you did not believe my words"—Z'khar'yah needed to keep his big, dumb, doubting thoughts to himself.

Z'khar'yah had asked God for help for his childless wife, and God had responded by sending a Messenger from His own heavenly presence. But all Z'khar'yah could see were the perceived obstacles of his earthly reality. When he reminded the Messenger of those obstacles—because, obviously, God must have forgotten them—it was received by God as audacity and ungratefulness. For all of his commendable attributes, Z'khar'yah nonetheless found himself silenced for resisting divine intervention.

When we fail to take God at His word, all our righteousness, blamelessness, obedience and service become absolutely meaningless. By relying too heavily on such things to measure our walk with God, we can easily be misled, thinking we know ADONAI better than we actually do. It might make us feel better to try to handle God and help Him figure out and deal with our issues, but it only proves our misperceptions about who's really in charge. The Father can see our obstacles just fine without our help, and He isn't threatened by them one bit.

Let us be righteous and blameless, not so that we may assume jurisdiction in heavenly matters, but so that we may find peace in the presence of God. Let us be open to divine surprises, and prepared to believe whatever our Master says...

PRAYER

ADONAI, I praise Your awesome Name and the power of Your might! Confound my reason, God, and send the miraculous to reveal my responsiveness to You. Let me not count on my outward acts as if they always reflect my inner self. I am beyond grateful, Abba, that You see, hear and answer my need; now teach me to always and immediately believe Your word...

MAKING GOOD FRUIT

> Then he said to the crowds coming to be immersed by him, "Brood of vipers! Who prompted you to flee from the coming wrath? Therefore, make fruits worthy of the reformation, and do not begin to say within yourselves, 'We have a father: אַבְרָהָם, Av'raham.' For I say to you that God is able—out of these stones—to raise *up* children to אַבְרָהָם, Av'raham. And the axe is already also laid to the root of the trees. Therefore, every tree not making good fruit is cut down, and it is thrown into fire."
>
> –LUKE 3:7-9

When people are coming to you for immersion and the release of sins, it's generally considered poor form to impugn their motives and call them a bunch of snakes. Yet this is exactly what Yochanan the Immerser did without apology—something, perhaps, we might consider when warning others of the dangerous sinfulness they are in.

Yochanan proclaimed an immersion of reformation—of turning from one's sins. When the crowds came to him, he got in their faces, challenging and warning them that immersion would not provide them with a magical cloak of love and salvation, but that the immersion *must* be followed by the making of good fruit that is worthy of reformation—fruit which demonstrates that one has left his sinful ways in the water. Yochanan was crystal clear regarding the results of an empty immersion: "And the axe is already also laid to the root of the trees. Therefore, every tree not making good fruit is cut down, and it is thrown into fire."

When we approach God, looking for forgiveness and salvation, no paternal pedigree or sacramental rite or canned prayer or emotional proclamation of repentance or amount of congregational meeting attendance is enough to save us. The life of Messiah in us must follow, evidencing a changed life. Unfortunately, we are a generation of soaking wet initiates with no intent—and no idea—how to daily follow through on our salvation. We bear the Name, but not the fruit.

The axe is ready, hovering above our roots. Now is the time for us all to shed our sin, take seriously our salvation, and purpose ourselves to produce good fruit… or risk falling into the fire. How fruity for Yeshua are you today? Make sure that it's good. Make sure that it's worthy of His Name…

PRAYER

ADONAI, I believe in the coming wrath, and I confess: I want to be saved from the fire. But Father, let my motivation for immersion and salvation not simply be to escape the flames, but because I want to give my whole life—every part of me—to the service of Your Son. I praise You, Master Yeshua, for the gift of unending Life! Make me a true believer; worthy to receive Your gift, as I devote myself to making good fruit for You.

WHAT WE ARE MADE OF

> And it came to pass... *that* יֵשׁוּעַ, Yeshua *was* also being immersed. And *while He was* praying, the heaven was opened, and the רוּחַ הַקֹּדֶשׁ, Ruach Ha-Qodesh came down upon Him in a bodily form, as if a dove. And a voice came out of heaven: "You are My Son—the Beloved. In You I delighted." [And] יֵשׁוּעַ, Yeshua, full of the רוּחַ הַקֹּדֶשׁ, Ruach HaQodesh, returned from the יַרְדֵּן, Yar'den and was brought in the רוּחַ, Ruach into the desert, being tempted *for* forty days by the Accuser. –LUKE 3:21-22, 4:1-2A

Yeshua arose from His water immersion only to face a baptism by *temptation*. The Ruach had descended upon Him, and the Father had audibly expressed His delight, but the Son's initiation was only just beginning. The Messiah was to be tempted in the desert for forty days by the Accuser—brought out by the Ruach to be *tested* there by God.

The Accuser proceeded to do his worst: "If You are *the* Son of God, [turn] this stone [into] bread...." "If You bow before me *in worship*... I will give to You... authority [and] glory...." (4:3-7). Famished from fasting, the Master still had the presence of mind to meet every poke and prod with the perfect response. Though the Accuser attempted to appeal to vanity, greed and lust for power—though he tried to make the Master doubt Himself and defend His identity, His authority and the very core of His being—for all his efforts, he would get nothing back in return but the word of God.

By leading Yeshua into the desert to go up against the Accuser, God was administering the Master's final test before presenting Him to the world. He not only allowed *but orchestrated* the Accuser's unfettered access to His Son so that His readiness could be both tested and proved. Likewise, we too, as disciples of Messiah, are sometimes thrust by God into times of testing. Yet when God tests us, it's not just to find out how far we have to go, but—as He did with His Son—to prove to us exactly how far we have come.

The Master was full of the Ruach HaQodesh and the word of God, fully prepared to fulfill His destiny. Weakened and depleted, He had faced the Accuser himself, and had come through the repeated and enticing temptations unscathed. We too have a destiny to fulfill and an Accuser to send running. Have you fully submitted your will to the Father and immersed yourself in His word? The times of testing are coming... so what will they prove that you're made of?

PRAYER

O God, Your times of testing can be painful and hard, but nothing I cannot endure when You are with me. I praise You, ADONAI, for Your wisdom and love; You see deeply into my innermost being. Test me, Father, that I may see myself through Your eyes, and lay bare to me the ways that I am weak or stubborn or strong. Thank You, Master, for showing me not only the distance I have left to go, but for proving to me just how far You've already brought me along...

HOLEY, HOLEY, HOLEY

> And He also spoke an analogy to them: "No one puts a patch torn from new clothing on old clothing; otherwise, then the new *cloth* will also make a tear, and the patch that *is* from the new *cloth* will not agree with the old." –LUKE 5:36

Our clothes—ourselves—are holey; that is, we're full of holes. It's not just from wear and tear—it's rips and splits and snags. The holes are remnants of places we shouldn't have been, things we shouldn't have done, and words we shouldn't have said— along with the damage that was left behind. It's a uniform of obstinance; a badge of pride; a costume of foolishness.

Yet rather than seek a new garment, we tend to only want mending from the Master. The old clothing is comfortable, cozy and familiar. For the most part, we love our old apparel— our old lives—and just want to keep on wearing it, wrapping ourselves in its false sense of contentment. We only want to patch up the holes and cover our brokenness enough that we might appear presentable to those who don't examine us too closely.

The Master teaches us, "No one puts a patch torn from new clothing on old clothing; otherwise, then the new *cloth* will also make a tear, and the patch that *is* from the new *cloth* will not agree with the old." Whether we have known Yeshua for only a short time, or we have been walking with Him for a while, the reason we end up slipping back into our old patterns and ways is because we never really removed our old clothes in the first place. We have been taking from God piecemeal, trying to sew up the cuts and tears, and ending up only making things worse. The old "us" before Yeshua and the new "us" in Messiah will always be at odds with one another... they will never agree.

Yeshua wants to entirely replace your wardrobe today. Stop trying to patch yourself up with little bits of Yeshua while you hold on to your old thinking, your old patterns, and your old ways—it will never work. God has a new garment for you, but only if you're really willing to wear it, and to get rid of the old one for good. It's time to let God take off your old holey self and clothe you again in something—and as someone—completely and totally new.

PRAYER

Master Yeshua, I confess: I'm still so full of holes! Forgive me for trying to match You up with the shredded garment of my old self and old ways. I praise You, ADONAI, for You have made me new clothes that are nothing like the rags I have loved and refused to discard. Help me today, Abba, to be willing to step out of my old garments, and to get rid of them forever—never returning to their deceptive familiarity and comfort. Cover me, God, in the purity and goodness of my new clothes—my new self—which You have been patiently waiting for me to wear...

HOPING FOR NOTHING

> "But love your enemies, and do good, and lend, hoping for nothing in return, and your reward will be great, and you will be sons of the Highest, because He is kind to the ungrateful and evil."
> –LUKE 6:35

It's really hard to like—much less love—people with opposing ideological views who despise your very existence. Really hard. Like, really, really, really hard. It is difficult—especially when we find their positions not only offensive, misguided, and wrong, but extremely depraved, dangerous and destructive—to not become livid and see the person promoting those views as anything but evil. And how do you love evil?

Yet as followers of Messiah, we are supposed to rise above our feelings. The Master tells us to love our enemies, do good to those hating us, bless those cursing us, and pray for those falsely accusing us. But all that is pretty much impossible to do if we're filled with rage and hatred toward them. We have to somehow let it go. We have to do more than just love those who love us back—indeed, even "the sinful ones" on the so-called "other side" are capable of that. No, we have to love those who revile us, and do good to them… and then hope for absolutely nothing in return. Because if the Father can be kind to the ungrateful and the evil, so must we.

Yes, it is easier said than done. Yes, we must tamp down our emotions and see our enemies as fellow human beings, rather than the putrid, vile incarnation of immorality, perversity and evil that they appear to be. Somewhere in there—lost inside that empty, miserable soul—is still a person like us… a person who may not be beyond saving. Even a mindless tool of the devil can still be reached by the goodness of God—no matter how high the likelihood of their rejection of Him, and of us. Yet who but God can say?

Our flesh may not like it, but loving our enemies and doing good to those who hate us is still the way of the Master. Particularly as the agents of enmity exponentially increase, we cannot debase the image and name of God by emulating their hostility and losing ourselves to that void. The way of Messiah is to love even those who would harm us for our innocence and our unselfish, good actions. We must not forget that our reward and sonship are not of this world—so neither should be our love…

PRAYER

Master Yeshua, teach me how to love my enemies by reminding me that I was once Your enemy. All that they threaten, Abba, I entrust to You—please keep my loved ones from harm. When I fight back and resist, O God, let me temper my rage with compassion, goodness and love. Help me, Father, to see all who bear Your image as You see them—to do good to them, though they may never do good to me.

TO WHOM LITTLE IS FORGIVEN

> "Therefore, I say to you, her many sins have been forgiven, because she loved much; but to whom little is forgiven, little does he love." –LUKE 7:47

Surely, most people have a distorted, inaccurate, and incomplete view of Yeshua. They really have no idea that He came to save us from our sins. One would think, though, that when presented with this news, people would leap at the chance to have all their sins forgiven, and then to receive eternal life. But they don't. Some will say it's nonsense. Some will say we're just trying to impose our "religion" on them. But the real resistance comes from the fact that they perceive no value in what's being offered. After all, what's there to love about being set free from sin if you don't believe you're sinful?

Though we all naturally know it is there, it can be difficult to admit our sin. It's embarrassing. It's deflating. It doesn't make us feel nice and happy inside. But when we hide our sin, or pretend that our thoughts and words and actions are not really sinful, then we become self-loathing and increasingly resistant to and distant from God... and this is true of believers, too.

When we do not admit and confess our sins, then we cannot receive forgiveness for them, and we will have no love in our hearts for Yeshua. But the more we love Yeshua, the more forgiveness we will receive, and the light cast on our sins will no longer yield shame, but gratefulness.

Don't limit your love for God by letting your sin go unaddressed. Take a good look at yourself, admit and confess your sin, and then be filled with overflowing love for God as you realize the true value and depth of His forgiveness.

PRAYER

God of the universe, Maker of all, I humble myself before You. Help me to grasp in the depths of my being the immeasurable value of Your unending forgiveness. Reveal to me, Father, the sins of my mind, my mouth, my hands and my feet—their seriousness, and what it truly means to have my slate wiped clean. Cast Your light deep in my soul, Master, and forgive my many sins, that I may pour back out to You in over-abounding freedom and love...

DENY YOURSELF

> And He said to all *of them*, "If anyone wants to come after Me, let him deny himself, and take up his *execution* stake daily, and follow Me; for whoever wants to save his life will lose it, and whoever loses his life for My sake, he will save it; for what is a man benefited, having gained the whole world, yet having lost or having forfeited himself?"
> –LUKE 9:23-25

When the Master came proclaiming the Reign of God and healing the sick and the infirmed, He brought wholeness and completeness to people's lives—they benefited because they had encountered the Messiah. But for those who would then choose to follow Him—to take their relationship with God more seriously—there was another step. Indeed, Yeshua did not bring wholeness merely to make their lives better; He was making them ready to become His disciples.

Many believers in Yeshua today stop prematurely in their relationship with Him. We seek Him out and pursue Him for how He can improve our lives, but when we finally catch up with Him—and He touches us, and He changes us—we simply thank Him very kindly, and then return to our previous heading…

…but that was never His plan.

The Master is calling us today: "If anyone wants to come after Me, let him deny himself." Yeshua didn't come to make your life better. He came so that you would completely give it up. It is not our life that He wants us to live, but His. He didn't sacrifice Himself so that He could occupy some small corner of ourselves, but so that we would voluntarily snuff out our own existence, and then fill ourselves up unconditionally with Him.

Today is the day to leave yourself behind and let Yeshua occupy you completely. Will you strip away and set aside all your wants, hopes, dreams, comforts, preferences and desires, and instead consume yourself with Messiah? What do you have to lose but your life? What do you have to gain but Yeshua?

PRAYER

Master Yeshua, I deny myself today—and tomorrow, and each day after that—so that I may truly follow You. Heal me and make me whole—not so that I may continue my life, but so that I may be made ready to lose it. Save me, Father, that I may live forever in selfless service of Your perfect Son. Help me seek to secure not merely a better and eternal life, but a life void of myself, and filled completely and only with You...

WHAT ARE YOU WAITING FOR?

> And [Yeshua] said to another, "Be following Me."
> And he said, "Sir, permit me, having gone away, to
> first bury my father." And He said to him, "Allow
> the dead to bury their own dead; but you, hav-
> ing gone away, publicize the Reign of God." And
> another also said, "I will follow you, sir, but first
> permit me to say good-bye to those in my house."
> And יֵשׁוּעַ, Yeshua said to him, "No one having put
> the hand on a plow, and looking back, is fit for the
> Reign of God." –LUKE 9:59-62

Yeshua's reactions sometimes seem incredibly harsh and in-
sensitive. To the man who said he would follow Him, but
wanted first to say goodbye to his family, the Master essentially declared that he was unfit for the Reign of God. And to
another man who asked to first bury his father, the Master—
apparently heartless—replied, "Allow the dead to bury their
own dead." What kind of a response is that?

If a part of us bristles at these exchanges, it's understand-
able. The men appear to have legitimate reasons for wanting
to delay following Yeshua. Let's give them the benefit of the
doubt and assume they actually care for their families and
want to communicate and demonstrate their love before leaving them behind—possibly indefinitely. Anyone with a heart
and a brain can appreciate that kind of sentiment. So what is
Yeshua's problem?

The Master responded in these instances with an exactly pro-
portionate amount of antagonism that would reflect the men's
true, inward animosity toward answering the call. While they

were saying with their lips, "I will follow," in their hearts they were saying, "but I love this more than I love You." When is it ever wrong to love your family? When that "love" is greater than our love for God. Our reasoning minds don't care for this arrangement at all, and therein lies the problem: we think we know better than God.

Having a pretext with God does you no good. If you truly want to follow Yeshua, first, be honest (with God and yourself) about your motives and intentions, and second, love nothing over Him. You will never fail to adequately love and care for your family if you first love and wholly pursue Yeshua.

What excuses are you offering Yeshua today? How harshly will He reply? The Master is calling out to you right now. Will you hesitate... or follow?

PRAYER

My Master, am I Your willing slave? Or am I just saying what I think You want to hear? Have I truly—and immediately—answered Your call? Or have I only made excuses to remain among the dead? Forgive me, Yeshua, for finding "legitimate" ways to avoid the sacrifice of actually following You and publicizing Your great Name. I hear You calling now, and I am committed to answer. No more excuses, Master... here I come!

COMFORTING WORDS, HARD WORDS

> "And I say to you, my friends: be not afraid of
> those *who are* killing the body, and after these
> things are not having anything more to do. But
> I will show you whom you should fear: fear Him
> who, after the killing *of the body*, is having author-
> ity to throw *you* to the גֵּיהִנּוֹם, Geihinom. Yes, I say
> to you: fear Him. Are not five sparrows sold for
> two coins? Yet not one of them is forgotten before
> God. Rather, even the hairs of your head have all
> been numbered. Fear not! You are of more value
> than many sparrows." –LUKE 12:4-7

When we're looking for an encouraging word from God, we
generally prefer that He just get right to it. So we keep going
back to those little snippets of Scripture that we know will
not let us down. Unfortunately, this is not the way His word
actually works. Generally speaking, you have to wade through
a lot of strong, convicting talk before you get to the so-called
"good stuff." Perhaps this is the reason many of us don't make
a habit of actually reading the Scriptures: too much extrane-
ous seriousness! We want to be told that everything is going
to be okay without having to face the Real.

But real is exactly what Yeshua is giving us here. Do you—
My friends—want to be unafraid of those persecuting you
and killing the body? Good! BE AFRAID OF THE ONE
WITH THE AUTHORITY TO SEND YOU TO HELL!
Wow. Not exactly the rainbows and unicorns I was looking

for, but that certainly puts things into perspective. I *guess* I'm encouraged now??

The Master rarely delivers the word we were expecting or hoping to hear, but He always gives us the pure, life-giving truth. He does not sugar-coat the facts or avoid difficult and uncomfortable subjects—we do that just fine all by ourselves. Instead, we are expected to sit there and take it—to get the "bad news" first, as it were—because it's often the most practical part of the message. But the good news is that if we are patient, He will also not neglect to offer us those longed-for words of comfort, peace and hope:

My friend, since God has not forgotten the sparrows, neither has He forgotten you. The Creator of the Universe has literally numbered each hair on your head—He cares, and knows every single thing about you. Because of this unimpeachable fact, you never ever have to be afraid. Though you may be under threat—though you may feel completely and utterly unworthy—you are of innumerable, immeasurable, incalculable and infinite value to your eternal Father in Heaven.

Now wasn't that worth the wade?

PRAYER

ADONAI my God, I praise Your great Name, for You see me in my every need, and You never fail to answer. Thank You, Master, for constantly telling me what I need to know, especially when it's the last thing I really want to hear. Forgive me, Abba, for glossing over the hard words just so that I can foolishly attempt to soothe my own soul. I receive Your every word, Yeshua; speak the whole truth to me, bringing both the hardness and the comfort... I am listening.

RICH TOWARD GOD

> "And God said to him, 'Unthinking one! This *very* night they will require your soul from you, and what things did you prepare? To whom will they be *given?*' So *it is for* he who is treasuring up to himself, and is not rich toward God." –LUKE 12:20-21

The Master gave an analogy of a certain rich man who had a whole bunch of *stuff*—so much stuff that he didn't have room to store it. And he was so rich that he could afford to tear down his existing storehouses to build even bigger ones to hold even more of his stuff. He made plans for his stuff. He looked forward to how his stuff would sustain him in the years to come. His stuff was good, and he was good to his stuff. He had a lot of stuff, and he thought about his stuff—a lot.

Then he dropped dead. So much for his stuff.

In the analogy, God reveals to the rich man, just before he dies, that he had been preparing for the wrong eventuality. He was expending all his effort and multiplying all his riches in order to provide for himself in the future. If only he had realized the future beyond the only one he could see.

None of us knows how long we have to live, but we will all certainly meet our Maker one day—and what will we have to show for it? Will we have spent our lives slaving away so that we will be provided for in our old age? Or will we instead—aside from reasonable preparations for possible longevity—have expended ourselves as slaves in the service of our Master? Those of us who are rich toward God will receive our eternal treasure. Those of us who treasure up to ourselves will have nothing in the end.

Work, then. Work hard. But work for God, and not for yourself. Tear down the storehouses for your stuff, and build even bigger ones to store all that your life will produce for the Master. Only then will you *really* be prepared for the future.

So it is for he who is not treasuring up to himself, but is lavishly rich toward God...

PRAYER

Oh, Father, I am a stupid, unthinking one. How can I spend my life believing in and serving You, but then not trust You to care for me when I am old? Show me, ADONAI, how my preparation for the future must not come at the expense of completely expending myself for You today. Let my storehouse be stuffed full of my service for You, O God—an endless treasure laid up for me forever...

DO YOU THINK THAT I CAME TO GIVE PEACE?

> "Do you think that I came to give peace in the earth? No, I say to you, but rather division!"
>
> –LUKE 12:51

In our divided world, some will claim the love of Yeshua to validate their so-called tolerance and diversity. They say that Yeshua would endorse people loving whomever they want to love, living however they want to live, and accepting everyone just the way they are. They say that this is what the Bible teaches as the definition of love, and that believers in Yeshua who disagree are just hypocritical bigots.

Setting aside the fact that people who say this have likely never even read the Bible, the problem with this point of view is that they depict Yeshua in a way that is wholly inconsistent with who He is. The way Yeshua loves us is nothing like they describe. Yeshua's love unites us, yes, but it does so through *division*—Yeshua's love *divides* us from what is wrong or un-righteous, and *unites* us around Him.

This is why Yeshua said that He did not come "to give peace in the earth... but rather division." The Messiah's own stated purpose for becoming flesh and living among us was to *divide* people—to *separate* us—forcing us to decide whether we would follow Him or indulge ourselves. Yeshua's division provides us with a clear, unambiguous choice between loving God and loving what opposes Him... including what some call "tolerance" and "diversity."

It can be a difficult image of the Master to accept—but only to those who don't really know what the Scriptures say. Yeshua is a disrupter first and foremost, yet also a comforter for those who truly love Him. If we faithfully follow our Master, and pattern after Him both the way we love and the way we fight, we too will be divided from that which opposes God... and we will find peace and acceptance in the One who is incapable of leaving us the same way He found us.

PRAYER

Father in Heaven, Your ways are not my ways; Your thoughts are not my thoughts. You alone, ADONAI, are capable of bringing peace and unity through the division brought by the perfection of Your Son. Teach me, Yeshua, to walk in Your ways of love, tolerance and peace—never as redefined by society—and let me not cause undue division by my own fleshly deficiencies. Send Your separation, Master, to distinguish between right and wrong, and help me to follow, no matter the cost...

WHEN YOU HAVE DONE
ALL THE THINGS

> "Does [the master] have favor toward the slave because he did the things *he was* directed *to do?* So also, when you have done all the things you are directed *to do*, you *should* say, 'We are worthless slaves; *only* that which we owed to do, we have done.'" –LUKE 17:9-10

Yeshua asked his disciples a rhetorical question concerning a slave who was coming in from being out working the field: Would his master invite him to immediately sit down and eat? Or is it more likely that he would instruct the slave to first prepare his master's meal, and then after he was done serving, he could feed himself? The latter being the obvious answer, Yeshua continued: "Does [the master] have favor toward the slave because he did the things *he was* directed *to do?*" In other words, given that the slave is already well-treated, should the master show his slave any unusual goodwill or kindness just because the slave did his job?

It's a fair question—especially when we, as children of God, can often feel a certain sense of entitlement to God's unmerited favor. While we can and should rely on His goodwill and kindness toward us, that does not set aside our simultaneous responsibility to submit to Him and do as we're told. It was never part of the arrangement that we be permitted to accept our adoption as sons at the expense of our purchase as slaves. We must not obey, then, in order to warrant a reward, but because we recognize and revere our owner.

As disciples of Messiah, Yeshua is our Master, and we are His slaves. He gives us an easy yoke and a light load—He cares for us and treats us well. The Master's teaching to us, then, is that we are to be like that slave who came in from working the field, yet was still expected to serve the meal. When we have done all that the Master has directed us to do, we should not feel as if the work made us deserving of higher praise or greater rewards. Rather, since we are in the Messiah's debt, we are to say, "We are worthless slaves; *only* that which we owed to do, we have done."

Being Messiah-followers, we have the highest honor and greatest privilege to be slaves of the Master Yeshua. Our job, then, is simply to humbly do as He says—to work the field, to serve Him, and to do only that which He has directed us to do. Let us not work because of the expectation of finding favor, but instead consider ourselves "worthless," counting slavery to God as its own great reward...

PRAYER

Master Yeshua, thank You for making me Your slave! I praise You for rescuing me from sin's enslavement, that I may be free to be enslaved to You. Though You value me, Master, teach me to see myself as worthless, so I will not stray from You and follow my own way. May my desire be only to do just what You direct me to do—to be a good slave in Your service, and to serve only You.

WHY DO YOU CALL ME GOOD?

> And a certain ruler questioned Him, saying, "Good teacher, what *can I* do *so that* I will inherit life age-enduring?" And יֵשׁוּעַ, Yeshua said to him, "Why do you call Me good? No one *is* good, except One—God." –LUKE 18:18-19

The Scriptures teach us that Yeshua is God—that the Word, who is God, became flesh, and all the fullness of the Deity dwells bodily in Him. So why, then, when someone called Yeshua "good," did He refute that characterization, and say that only "God" is good? What in the world is that supposed to mean? God is good, but Yeshua—who is God—is not? So is He God, or isn't He?

Too often we confer characteristics on Yeshua that He Himself would disavow, especially when we conflate his full deity and complete humanity. Because the mystery of His existence is so deep and profound, we tend to over-simplify our understanding of Him, failing to appreciate the nuances of living inside such a paradox. As a flesh and blood human being with a specific mission to accomplish, Yeshua did not think being equal to God—a thing He possessed—to be a thing to hold onto. For all intents and purposes, He emptied and lowered Himself so that He could serve both God and man. And He was completely comfortable with and unconfused by that arrangement.

As disciples of Messiah, we also confer characteristics on ourselves that we ought not to assign. We conflate being saved with being holy or righteous, and fail to appreciate the nuances of living as a new creature inside our old, stinking flesh. Like the Master Yeshua, we must not claim a divine advantage as if our remaining time in the body has no meaning.

If Yeshua, who is God, humbled Himself so much that He refused even the description of being good, then how much more should we lower ourselves in our own eyes? As we ponder the mystery of the Messiah, let us also not over-simplify or ignore our own paradoxes, sacrificing our acceptance and understanding of one spiritual reality over another...

PRAYER

I praise You God, for Your unfathomable mysteries; help me to catch even a glimpse of Your truth! Teach me, Father, to see Your Son through *His* eyes, that I may better perceive myself. Show me, Master, where I am commingling my new life with the old, thereby rendering meaningless Your life in me. Let me not be satisfied with having the salvation that is not yet, but instead burn to walk in the holiness and righteousness that comes from the salvation that is now.

BLESSED IS HE WHO IS COMING

> And as He was now coming near, at the descent of the Mountain of the Olives, the whole crowd of the disciples began rejoicing to praise God with a loud voice for all the powerful acts they had seen, saying, "BLESSED *IS* HE WHO IS COMING, the King, IN THE NAME OF ADONAI! Peace in Heaven, and glory in the highest!" –LUKE 19:37-38

The people were hanging on His every word, following wherever He would go. When the Master entered Y'rushalayim riding on a colt, the whole crowd of disciples could not contain their joy, and began to loudly give praise to God for all the powerful acts they had seen. The P'rushiym, clearly agitated by this display, thought the disciples deserving of rebuke, and told Yeshua as much. But the Master replied, "I say to you that if these will be silent, the stones will cry out!" (19:40).

To ascribe such praise to Yeshua may imply a great deal about how He was perceived by the people: the refuge of ADONAI, God's strength and salvation, the rejected stone that had become head of a corner, the embodiment of God's steadfast love. If this is what the people were praising about, it's no wonder the P'rushiym were upset. How can you compete with a reality that has been bursting forth from the beginning of time?

And yet, we often manage to find a way to fill our lives with rivals to His praise. Worry, doubt, sadness and fear direct our attention away from His eternal magnificence, shutting up our mouths and shutting down our spirits. Our inability to recognize Him daily, due to our fundamental unfamiliarity with His word, leaves us numb—never to be overcome by the overwhelming, spontaneous impulse to praise. ADONAI's power is incomparable, but against such paralysis, who can win?

God's salvation and provision for us is so great—so enormous, so glorious—that His praise cannot be contained... except by a heart weighed down, or an unfruitful mind. If our daily response to God is silence, or our outward praise is filled with empty and routine platitudes, creation itself will find a way to replace us, and resound in declaration of His wonders.

Can your praise for Yeshua today out-praise a pile of rocks? Respond to Him for His salvation and powerful acts, and give ADONAI all the glory due His Name!

PRAYER

Yeshua! King! You have answered me and become my salvation! I praise You, O God, and glorify You by pouring out cries of adulation in response to Your strength, authority and power! Lift me up, Master, and fill me with joy, that I may return it to You in praise. May my voice ring out in abundant blessing of Your Name, and put every rock and stone to shame...

BE CAREFUL OF YOURSELVES

> "And be careful of yourselves, otherwise your hearts
> may be weighed down with crapulence and drunk-
> enness and *the* anxieties of life, and that day will
> come on you suddenly; for it will come as a snare
> on all those dwelling on the face of all the land *of
> the earth.* So be alert in every season, praying that
> you may have strength to escape all these things
> that are about to come to pass, and to stand before
> the Son of Man." –LUKE 21:34-36

The Master warned His disciples that great calamity and persecution were coming. Yet He also promised His protection,
the wisdom and words to refute oppressors, and the capacity
to persevere through distress and fear. Yeshua told them these
things so that they would be prepared whenever that Day
would come. He did not want them taken by surprise, but to
be able to recognize the signs that everything was about to
happen.

As so, in preparation for what lay ahead, the Master concluded
His words of warning by admonishing the disciples to also
"be careful of yourselves." Of all the things that would be
coming against them, the disciples were potentially their own
worst enemy.

Yeshua exhorted them not to become distracted by life. He
knew of man's tendency to lose both heart and patience while
waiting on a deferred promise—that we will sooner self-
medicate than we will pray for perseverance. Yeshua also understood people's frailty, and how forgetful and preoccupied
we can become in times of unrelenting stress. The Master did

not want His disciples to be so weighed down by anxiety that the Day would "come on [them] suddenly," and they would find themselves too weak in both spirit and body to escape.

God only knows what calamities and trying times await us, but if we do not remain "alert in every season," we too will be taken by surprise, and not have the strength to get away. Don't be distracted by your life. Don't seek to deaden the feelings you have toward your present circumstances—you will only succeed in weighing down your heart. Lift up your eyes to the Master daily, and wait for Him with patience, remembering that His time is not our time.

The Day is coming, so don't lose heart! Be patient, pray for strength, and get ready to behold the Son of Man…

PRAYER

Father in Heaven, please give me the strength to hold on and persevere. I trust You for the way of escape, Abba—but fill me with patience, that I may wait for You free from worry and anxiety. Teach my heart, Master, to not seek distractions of any kind, that I may not use them to try to fill the void. Help me to seek instead to fill my heart and mind only with You. I await You daily, Master… come, Yeshua, come…

REASONING WITH THE UNREASONABLE

> And Pilate, having called together the chief כֹּהֲנִים,
> Ko'haniym and the rulers and the people, said to
> them, "You brought this man to me as *one* turning
> away the people, and look! having examined *him*
> in your sight, I found no fault in this man in *regard*
> *to* those things you brought forward against him.
> No, neither *did* Herod, for he sent him back to us;
> and look! nothing worthy of death is having been
> done by him." –Luke 23:13-15

The crowd, led by the chief Ko'haniym, brought Yeshua to
Pilate for execution. When Pilate issued his verdict—"I find
no fault in this man"—the crowd simply grew "*all* the more
urgent" (23:5), and pressed Pilate for a different outcome.

Reiterating his finding, the people persisted, calling out,
"Crucify, crucify him!" To this, Pilate replied a third time,
"Why? What evil did he do? I find no cause for death in him."
Yet the people "were pressing *him* with loud voices, asking *for*
Him to be crucified, and their voices were prevailing" (23:21-
23).

"And *so* Pilate gave judgment for their request being done"
(23:24).

Though the Master's execution was necessary (for our sake),
it was nevertheless unjust, brought about by manipulation,
lies, and a host of raw, unchecked emotions. By the time the
people had been riled up—their basest emotions inflamed—
there was no reasoning with them. They would not engage

in civilized debate, but rather sought to scream their way to victory, demanding to have their way through incessant, unrelenting pressure against politicians afraid of losing power and control.

And two thousand years later, nothing has changed.

Are you being led around today, not by reason, but by your unreasonable emotions? Don't give in to your feelings—no matter how justified they may seem—while trying to get your way simply by being the shrillest, most insufferable voice in the room. Instead, crucify your flesh, and consider the consequences of your actions. Then let the peace and righteousness of Messiah rule—and in you, no fault will be found...

PRAYER

Adonai, is there anyone left who will not persist in destructive, emotional screed? Why can't we all progress toward rational, civilized discourse? No matter my feelings, Abba, help me to not get roped in to the mob mentality, leading with my flesh rather than my spirit. Teach me, Master, to be selective and careful about the voices I allow to influence me. Show me, Yeshua, where I too have been unreasonable and irrational, and help me to stop laying blame where no fault is deserved...

HE IS NOT HERE

> And upon their having become afraid and having inclined the faces to the ground, *the men* said to them, "Why do you look for the living among the dead? He is not here, but was raised!" –LUKE 24:5-6A

The women arrived at the Master's tomb, finding the entrance-stone rolled away, and Yeshua's body nowhere in sight. As they stood there, perplexed, two men in gleaming clothes were suddenly standing there, saying, "Why do you look for the living among the dead? He is not here, but was raised!" And the women remembered what Yeshua had said, and they went away to breathlessly tell the other disciples what had happened....

But that was then.

Today, almost 2,000 years later, the Body of Messiah is still standing in an empty tomb, perplexed, and searching for Yeshua. We have forgotten what the Master said; we are looking for the living among the dead.

This is where many of us keep God: relegated to a corner of our lives, kept in a box that we only open from time to time. Our thoughts are not consumed with how we might serve Him. We do not look to Him to tell us what to think, nor do we even consult Him for the decisions of our lives. We go on without Him, bluffing our way through, while there in our mind-grave He remains.

When, then, do we call on Him? When do we seek His face?

When we need something.

And so we cry out, expecting to find Him right where we left Him.

But He is not there.

Not in our box.

Our walk with Yeshua is indeed dead as long as we hold back any portion of our lives for ourselves. The Master didn't sacrifice Himself so that we could be our own masters. God didn't save us so that we would seek Him only when it's convenient or when we suddenly realize we're in trouble. God wants *all* of you—all your devotion, all your love, all your attention... all the time.

Why do you look for the living among the dead? Yeshua is waiting for you outside the tomb, inside the life that He alone has envisioned for you. So what are you waiting for? Go to Him, now and forever, and then follow everywhere He leads...

...and walk among the dead no more.

PRAYER

ADONAI, forgive me for trying to keep You in a box, as if anything can contain You. I have been lifeless and confused, thinking of You as my backup in case of emergency, rather than as the active leader and master of my life You truly are. Help me to remember, Father, that I will never find the living God entombed in my dead and empty walk. I want to live, Yeshua! I want to follow and serve! Make me alive again in You.

UNTHINKING AND SLOW IN HEART

> And [the two men recounted how] certain *ones* of [the disciples] went away to the tomb and found *it* even as the women said, but Him they did not see. And [Yeshua] said to them, "O unthinking and slow in heart to believe on all that the prophets spoke! Was it not necessary for the Messiah to suffer these things, and to enter into His glory?"
>
> −LUKE 24:24-26

The rumors were swirling: He's gone! The tomb is empty! They say they saw angels. Someone stole His body! Could He be... alive?

That day, two of Yeshua's disciples were traveling along the road when a stranger appeared. He walked with them, listening to them recount the incredible events surrounding their Master's disappearance. But for all their reasoning, the two could not make sense out of what had happened.

Then the stranger interjected, "O unthinking and slow in heart to believe on all that the prophets spoke!" And He explained to them everything the Scriptures said about the Messiah.

As the three of them broke bread together, the disciples' eyes were suddenly opened, and they recognized the stranger. It was Yeshua! He was alive! And the disciples said to one another, "Was not our heart burning within us as He was speaking to us on the road?" (24:32).

How often are we, too, as Yeshua's disciples, unthinking and slow in heart? We study the Scriptures, and we learn, and we think about things, and we reason them out, and we try to get our theology all bound up in a neat little package that we feel is manageable and doable and safe. But there's a big, huge part of thinking that we sometimes forget to do—the part where we are quick to believe with our heart the things we already know.

We know that the word of God is true, and we become certain of what we believe, *not* because we get it through our heads, but when we let God speak it to our hearts.

Be thinking and quick in your heart to believe God's glorious and impossible possibilities today. Perhaps you, too, are walking with a stranger, who—if you let Him—will set your heart ablaze.

PRAYER

O God, I want to believe! I want to hope and expect and have faith for what seems impossible. Help me, Father, to not accept the rumors of doubt, but to let my heart hear and believe the whispers of truth. Teach me, Yeshua, to not be so focused on the thoughts in my head that I forget to believe with my innermost being. Master, let my heart burn with confidence and joy and faith in Your resurrection power for me.

WE HEARD THEM SPEAKING

> And there appeared to them tongues *being* divided—as if of fire—and it sat upon each one of them. And they were all filled with the רוּחַ הַקֹּדֶשׁ, Ruach HaQodesh and began to speak with other languages, as the רוּחַ, Ruach was giving them to declare. And *during the Feast*, there were יְהוּדִים, Y'hudiym living in יְרוּשָׁלַיִם, Y'rushalayim—God-fearing men *who traveled* from every nation of those under the heaven—and at the sound of this having come… they were amazed and in wonder, saying, "…we heard them speaking in our languages the great things of God!" –ACTS 2:3-6A, 7A, 11B

From every nation under heaven, God-fearing Jews descended upon Y'rushalyim for the Feast. The Master Yeshua had been taken up into the sky, but His disciples continued to band together as they joined their fellow Jews in God's House. Suddenly, the sound of a driving, violent breath filled the Temple, and tongues of fire divided and sat upon each one of the disciples. "And they were all filled with the רוּחַ הַקֹּדֶשׁ, Ruach HaQodesh and began to speak with other languages." Confounded and amazed, the Jews said in wonder, "We heard them speaking in our languages the great things of God!" Then Keifa stood up among them and began to declare.

More than just a spectacle and a sign, the prophetic pouring out and filling of the Ruach empowered and emboldened Keifa and the disciples. The multi-lingual utterances did not shock the Jewish worshippers simply because they heard them in their own languages—no, the words the disciples were speaking were very specific: they were declaring the praises of God.

And when Keifa, the denier, stood up to answer the confusion, he was no longer confused about what he would stand up for—for the rest of his life. With boldness and authority, he connected Scripture after Scripture to demonstrate that the risen, ascended Yeshua is the Jewish Messiah.

We can be confident and bold in our knowledge of the word of God and the truth of Yeshua's Good News, but only by the outpouring of the Ruach HaQodesh can we be filled with the authoritative boldness to be an effective instrument of transformation in people's beliefs and lives.

Let us proclaim Yeshua, then, not simply with conviction, but empowered by the Ruach HaQodesh. Let us yield ourselves to His influence and leading, and open our hearts and minds not to counterfeit spirits, but to His authentic in-filling. May we boldly proclaim the Good News of Yeshua in power, with true authority, moored by the glory and guidance of God's perfect word...

PRAYER

God of Heaven, You alone are great! You do not leave Your people lost and in distress, but You answer with power and mystery! Pour out Your Ruach upon me, ADONAI—send Your signs, prophecies, dreams and visions. But most of all, fill me, Master, that I may speak with Your boldness, act in Your authority, and proclaim only Your word. You are amazing and wondrous, God most high; thank You for sending Your Ruach...

ALL THINGS IN COMMON

> And they were continuing steadfastly in the
> teaching of the emissaries and in the sharing,
> in the breaking of the bread and in the prayers.
> And *reverent* fear was coming on every soul, for
> many wonders, and also signs, were being done
> through the emissaries. And all those believing
> were together and had all things *in* common,
> and they were selling their properties and their
> possessions and were dividing them up to all, as
> anyone had need. –ACTS 2:42-45

The hundred and twenty had swelled to more than three
thousand in a single day. Then, without instruction—without
prodding—these brand new Messianic Jewish believers began
selling their possessions to help provide for the needy among
them. They shared everything they had, they continued to
meet together daily in the Temple, they gathered in each
other's homes, they had favor with the people, and they were
all of one mind. And "every day, the Master was adding together those being saved" (2:47).

What wouldn't you do to see that?

There is no doubt: something unique and unprecedented had
taken place. The Master Yeshua had just defeated death, the
Ruach HaQodesh had just been given, and 120 Jews had just
powerfully proclaimed the Good News such that 3,000 more
Jews were saved in a day. Brothers in blood—now brothers
again through the blood of the Messiah—were filled with
awe and joy, and responded by becoming a thriving Yeshua-
community overnight.

So what's stopping us from doing it too?

We can tell ourselves that we can't experience God in this way because back then was a special time, among a special people, for a unique purpose, under unique conditions.

So that means we can't try? It's not a Scriptural goal to which we should aspire? It wasn't meant to continue and spread?

The reason we don't seek and work toward this kind of community is either because we can't fathom it, because we're content with the way things are, or because we just don't believe it's necessary or possible. But in the beginning, this was the natural, organic result of people who knew God and understood the eternal thing He had done for them in Yeshua: to come together as family members of a brand new Household, with an insatiable appetite for God's word, His spirit, and one another.

Though it may seem like a pipe dream, it will only and ever remain a dream as long as we refuse to change our situations, and deny the need to challenge ourselves...

So what are we waiting for?

PRAYER

Adonai my God, did You merely do something unprecedented 2,000 years ago? Or did You also set a precedent that Your children have largely rejected? Teach me, Abba, to not be content with the way things are—to not make excuses for why things can't ever be different or better. Ignite my heart, Master, for the true togetherness of a real, biblical Yeshua-community—and for the resulting daily addition of those being saved.

WE CANNOT HELP BUT SPEAK

> But כֵּיפָא, Keifa and יוֹחָנָן, Yochanan, answering, said
> to them, "Whether it is righteous in the sight of
> God to listen to you rather than to God, you *be the*
> judge, for we cannot *help* but speak what we saw
> and heard." –Acts 4:19-20

Keifa and Yochanan had been taken into custody because the
Jewish authorities had been "greatly annoyed" (4:2) by their
teaching that Yeshua had risen from the dead. As they stood
before the Sanhedrin, Keifa proceeded to answer the inter-
rogation with the message of salvation through Yeshua—that
"there is no other Name under the heaven… in which we must
be saved" (4:12). Frustrated by this response, the Sanhedrin
commanded the emissaries to no longer teach in Yeshua's
Name. To this they defiantly replied, "Whether it is righteous
in the sight of God to listen to you rather than to God, you
be the judge, for we cannot *help* but speak what we saw and
heard." Reluctantly, they were let go.

What was it that drove these two, simple men? How were they
able to boldly and audaciously face likely imprisonment and
oppression, much less continue to dig a hole for themselves by
not keeping their mouths shut? Did they have a death wish?
Perhaps they were just insane. Or maybe they were driven by
something far greater than fear—even greater than fervor and
zeal. Maybe, deep inside themselves, they had been funda-
mentally rearranged so that, no matter how hard they tried to
stay quiet, they just couldn't help themselves.

These days, it is becoming increasingly difficult to publicly
speak what we believe. Or is it? It's true that the tenor of our

society is making it harder and harder to proclaim our faith and beliefs without fear of reprisal. But if we are truly driven by the Ruach, and committed to—and unashamed of—what we believe and Who we serve, then we will literally not be able to "*help* but speak." Neither our reasoning mind nor our physical body will be capable of holding us back—regardless of fear, regardless of consequences.

If comfortable societal temperatures are what empower and embolden you to proclaim Yeshua, then it's long past time to reassess your relationship with God. Do you truly believe in the faith of the Messiah Yeshua? Then don't listen to people's threats rather than listening to God. Submit your mind and your will completely to the Master, and then relinquish control of your mouth to the Ruach… and speak.

PRAYER

Father, I have been afraid—afraid of feeling uncomfortable, of confrontation, of retaliation, and of real consequences. I *do* believe in You, Master, but I have become too accustomed to staying silent. Fill me, Ruach HaQodesh—help me to subdue my flesh, and drive me to bring forth Your truth. Make me deaf, ADONAI, to the threats of this world, that I may speak what I have seen and heard, and resist You no more.

IN THE STRETCHING
OUT OF YOUR HAND

> [They] lifted up the voice to God with one mind and said, "[Both] Herod and Pontius Pilate were gathered together… with גּוֹיִם, Goyim and peoples of יִשְׂרָאֵל, Yis'rael against Your holy servant יֵשׁוּעַ, Yeshua… to do whatever Your hand and Your purpose predetermined to come to pass. And now, ADONAI, look on their threatenings and give to Your slaves to speak Your word with all freedom, in the stretching out of Your hand, for healing and signs and wonders to come to pass through the Name of Your holy servant—יֵשׁוּעַ, Yeshua!" –ACTS 4:24A,27-30

After Keifa and Yochanan had been released from the Sanhedrin's custody, they rejoined their friends and recounted the oppression they had endured. This event made it clear that the persecution of the Master, which had begun under the likes of Herod and Pilate, would continue with them—a mantle and fate they faithfully received. So in response, everyone began to pray, lifting up their voices to God "with one mind."

And yet, realizing that they now faced threats and plots against them for teaching and proclaiming the Name of Yeshua, the disciples did not ask God for protection. They did not ask for the defeat of those Gentile and Jewish leaders set against them, nor did they ask for victory over their oppressors. They prayed for nothing that would help keep them from harm or prevent their inevitable persecution. Instead, they asked God to give them the words that they should boldly speak, and that through the Name of Yeshua would come healing, signs and wonders.

As disciples of Messiah, the first response to threats against us because of our faith should be neither to mount a defense nor to launch an offensive, but rather to ask God for words, signs and wonders. This is how the people of Israel were set free from Egypt. This is how the Messiah Yeshua turned the world upside down. As ADONAI stretches out His hand to fulfill His predetermined purpose, our prayer should not simply be for the defeat of God's enemies, but that we may actively operate in concert with His will to confront the darkness and save the world.

Let us be bold in our faith and filled with the Ruach, such that our walk with Messiah may invite danger and even persecution. But then, as we face our fate, let us neither cower in fear nor assail in vengeance, but rather speak with all freedom the words of light and life. ADONAI has a purpose for us: to be His mouth and hands and feet—to be the instruments of His will upon the earth. Let us pray that by a mighty display of power, God's will may be done through us, and the Name of His holy servant Yeshua may be glorified!

PRAYER

Abba, Father, strengthen my faith and my walk, that I might be found worthy of threats and plots against me. ADONAI, "do whatever Your hand and Your purpose predetermine to come to pass"—no matter what the cost I may endure. Master, give to me—Your slave—to speak Your word with all boldness and freedom. And "in the stretching out of Your hand," O God, let Your "healing and signs and wonders come to pass through" me, in "the Name of Your holy servant—יֵשׁוּעַ, Yeshua!"

NOT ABLE TO WITHSTAND

> And the Twelve [said], "It is not pleasing that we, having left *the service of* the word of God, *have to* serve at tables. So, brothers, look for seven men from among you... whom we might set over this necessity...." [A]nd they chose Stephen.... And there arose certain of those of the synagogue called "of the Freedmen," and Cyrenians, and Alexandrians, and of those from Cilicia and Asia, disputing with Stephen, but they were not able to withstand the wisdom and the רוּחַ, ruach with which he was speaking. –Acts 6:2-5,9-10

One might think that Stephen was a little over-qualified to be a waiter, yet he was exactly the kind of man the Twelve were looking for. The job? Food service. The qualifications? Being well testified of, and full of the Ruach HaQodesh and wisdom. Stephen also happened to be full of faith, unmerited favor and power, and he was doing great wonders and signs among the people. He was a really, really good waiter.

As the word of God increased and the number of disciples multiplied exceedingly, several factions began to arise in the synagogue, and a dispute broke out between them and Stephen. Presumably being challenged over his beliefs, or perhaps over the disciples' soaring numbers, Stephen responded by serving up a whole lot more than a plate full of falafel and hummus. Indeed, "they were not able to withstand the wisdom and the רוּחַ, ruach with which he was speaking." So they falsely accused him, and dragged him before the Sanhedrin.

When we find ourselves disputing with unbelievers about our faith, nothing would be sweeter than to blow our opposers' minds with wise and spiritual words. Yet such an ability is not acquired through learning and education, but rather by the ravenous consumption of the spiritual food that is God's word. It comes not through the accumulation of religious knowledge, but as a result of our character built through submission to the Spirit. Who we have become in and through Messiah—not clever rhetoric—is what confounds and persuades the mind of the unbeliever.

Let us, then, seek to speak with wisdom and power, not standing against the Ruach HaQodesh and communicating out of our own reasoning. Instead, we must stand firm in God's unmerited favor, and be people of godly character who will declare only what the Spirit instructs us to say. As servants of God, we too need to be full of the Spirit, fed only by the pure nourishment of His word. So be diligent to qualify to do God's spiritual work, and then accept your humble recruitment into the labor of His eternal service.

PRAYER

Adonai my God, put Your words in my mouth, that my opposers may not withstand the wisdom and the ruach with which I speak. Fill me with Your Ruach, Adonai, and with faith and power, that I may be a mighty vessel for Your truth. But more than that, Abba, make me a person of integrity and good reputation, that my words and my walk will testify only of You. Humble me, Master, that in Your merciful, unmerited favor I may be found worthy to enter not only Your presence, but the glory of Your service forever.

AMAZED OR CHANGED?

> And a certain man by *the* name שִׁמְעוֹן, Shim'on was previously in the city using magic and amazing the גּוֹיִם, Goyim of שֹׁמְרוֹן, Shom'ron, saying himself to be a certain great one, to whom they were all paying attention, from small to great, saying, "This one is the Power of God who is called Great." And they were paying attention to him because of his having amazed them for a long time with deeds of magic. –ACTS 8:9-11

A certain man named Shim'on had been using magic to amaze the people of Shom'ron. The entire city, great and small, was paying attention to him—so much so that they were saying, "This one is the Power of God who is called Great." But when Philip came along (the server, not the emissary) proclaiming the Name of Yeshua, all the people believed the Good News regarding the Reign of God—including Shim'on.

Keifa and Yochanan soon came to Shom'ron, and when they prayed and laid hands on the people, the new believers received the Ruach HaQodesh. But when Shim'on the magician saw that the Ruach was given through the laying on of hands, he offered the emissaries money, hoping he could acquire that same power and authority. This caused Keifa to explode with a stinging rebuke: Shim'on was fit for "destruction," his heart was not right before God, he possessed "wickedness," and was in "the bile of bitterness," and the "bond of unrighteousness" (8:20-23).

Shim'on the magician brought a lot of baggage with him to the faith, but it was the importance he placed on the superficial that ultimately brought him down. No doubt, God's amazing power has been known to be visible and spectacular. But Shim'on's mistake was believing that the outward manifestation was the power itself. He did not realize—or would not accept—that the external was simply evidence of something deeper that God was powerfully doing.

Let us not be so quickly desirous of and easily amazed by outward displays of power—indeed, they may just be someone's sleight of hand. Instead, let us remember that the purpose of the outward is not to enthrall and amaze, but to bring about deep and lasting change in our inward ways.

PRAYER

Magnificent and awesome God, I magnify and praise Your Name! Teach me by Your Ruach to be discerning, and to not be taken in by counterfeit or contrived displays of power. Let my heart be right before You, ADONAI, not bound in unrighteousness or bitterness—not seeking You only superficially. Rather, free me, Master, to receive Your Ruach in deep humility, and to be truly amazed by the inward change You are doing in me.

ACCEPTABLE TO HIM

> And כֵּיפָא, Keifa, having opened his mouth, said,
> "I take hold of the truth that God is no accepter of
> faces, but in every ethnic group, he who is fearing
> Him and is putting righteousness into action is
> acceptable to Him." –Acts 10:34-35

Keifa was hungry. While he was waiting for his meal, he
had no idea that—the day before—God had set in motion
a series of events that would change the world forever. As
Keifa's destiny approached from the road below, he was on the
house-top praying, when he had the most perplexing vision
from God (10:9ff). Why would he—a Jew—be told to kill
and eat forbidden, unclean animals? Of course! Now he didn't
have to wait for dinner! He could just make himself a ham
sandwich! Hmm. Perhaps not.

While Keifa was pondering all this, the Ruach told him to
go downstairs and follow the men who had come for him.
They had been sent as a result of another vision given to man
named Cornelius—who, it turns out, was a righteous, praying, God-fearing, *Italian.* It was "illicit" in Jewish culture to
keep company with Gentiles, so by the time Keifa arrived
at Cornelius' house, he was pretty sure this wasn't about a
sandwich.

Keifa proceeded to share the message of Yeshua with Cornelius' house, and the Ruach HaQodesh fell on the Gentiles
there, even as He had on the Y'hudiym nearly a decade earlier
(Acts 2). This sealed the true meaning of the vision: that a
righteous person, regardless of ethnic group or nation, is
neither unclean nor unholy, but fully acceptable to God.

In giving Keifa the jarring, curious vision, God stirred up Keifa's heart and mind to begin to think differently regarding his long-held preconceived ideas—the kind of ideas we all tend to have. So what kind of divine intervention is it going to take to get you to see *your* own biases, misconceptions and, especially, your wrong-headed theology?

Fear God and put his righteousness into action, and then pray that He opens your eyes today.

PRAYER

I praise and fear You, ADONAI; teach me to never pridefully call unholy anything or anyone You have cleansed. Humble me, God, and reveal to me how I have been stuck in my thoughts and ways. Grab my attention, Master—astonish me! —and knock loose in my mind and spirit the things that are keeping me stubborn and blind. Make me holy and acceptable in Your sight, Father, that I may only see with the vision of righteousness.

TO REMAIN FAITHFUL

> And they sent out בַּר־נַבָּא, Bar-Naba to go through to Antioch, who, having come and having seen the *unmerited* favor of God, was rejoicing and was exhorting all with purpose of heart to remain faithful to the Master. –ACTS 11:22B-23

Following the death of Stephen, an oppression of the believers in Y'hudah began. Though they were scattered throughout the region, from Phoenicia to Cyprus to Antioch, they continued to speak the word—but only to other Y'hudiym. Some of the believers, however, ventured out, and proclaimed the Good News of Yeshua also to the Hellenists—Jews who had assimilated into the Greek culture in which they lived. Amazingly, a great number of the Hellenists also believed, and they turned to the Master.

Word of this made it back to Y'rushalayim, so they dispatched Bar-Naba. Once in Antioch, Bar-Naba witnessed "the *unmerited* favor of God"—that these broken-off branches, who had rejected their Jewishness, were returning to ADONAI through the Messiah Yeshua. God had not forgotten or forsaken them. When Bar-Naba saw this, he "was rejoicing and was exhorting all with purpose of heart to remain faithful to the Master." And "a great many were added to the Master" (11:24).

Like the Hellenists who fully assimilated into alien cultures, hiding from their true identity in ADONAI, believers in Messiah also face the danger of falling prey to foreign lures. The world we inhabit, being geared toward convenience and gratification, efficiently baits us into rejecting our own values and distinctions in Messiah. We are, then, barely effective in reaching our communities for Yeshua because we ourselves become barely distinguishable from the unbelieving people around us. As Messiah-followers, we must not fit in, but rather "remain faithful to the Master," and stay true to who we really are: set apart, in Messiah.

Have you remained faithful to the Master? Or do you look and act much like the world? Have you been championing the truth of God's word? Or have you substituted your faith for something that only slightly resembles it? Today is the day to separate yourself to God in Messiah, and, with purpose of heart, be different.

PRAYER

ADONAI, I have not been discriminating between the holy and the worldly. I do and say very little in my normal, everyday life that sets me apart as Your child. Help me, Master, to evaluate how I behave and spend my time in order to see how much I actually look like world. Teach me, Yeshua, what it truly means to be different, and what I must change to remain faithful to You.

THE RIGHT WAYS
OF THE MASTER

> "O *you* full of all underhandedness and all un-
> scrupulousness! son of the Accuser! enemy of all
> righteousness! Will you not stop perverting the
> right ways of the Master?" –ACTS 13:10

Paul and Bar-Naba had been sent out from Antioch, and soon found themselves going through the island of Paphos proclaiming the word of God. The proconsul there also desired to hear the word, so he called for the two emissaries. When they arrived, they found a magian—that is, some kind of sorcerer or magician—named Elymas there with the proconsul. Elymas outwardly opposed the emissaries, "seeking to pervert the proconsul from the faith" (13:8).

Paul, then, filled with the Ruach, said to Elymas, "'Will you not stop perverting the right ways of the Master? And now... be blind!...' And instantly, a... darkness fell on [Elymas]; and he, going around, was looking for someone to lead *HIM* by the hand" (13:10b-11). Then the proconsul, having seen what had happened, "believed, being astonished at the teaching of the Master" (13:12).

Like many people, the proconsul was seeking the spiritual and, being undiscerning, was willing to entertain any voice and any influence. Yet as soon as he invited in the voice of the Master, the Ruach actively set about keeping him from being dissuaded from the faith.

As disciples of Messiah, we too—like Paul—need to not only be prepared to "teach" unbelievers this way of the Master, but to be spiritually discerning within ourselves. We need to know God not with head knowledge and doctrines, or with extravagant yet counterfeit spirits, but through the power and the guidance of the Ruach of Truth.

Every unbeliever has already opened himself up to the spiritual world in some way. We need to be ready, then, not just to defend and promote our faith, but to spiritually fight for their souls. No magic is any match for the authority of the Ruach HaQodesh... are you ready to wield it?

PRAYER

Father, I know that there are spiritual forces actively working to pervert the faith and discourage people's belief. Teach me, Master, how to not fight only with the word of truth, but with the power of the Ruach HaQodesh. Help me, Yeshua, to see with spiritual eyes, that I may discern how others (and perhaps even myself) have been made spiritually susceptible. Fill me, ADONAI, with boldness and understanding, that I may reach into—and help rescue Your children from—their blind, spiritual worlds.

WHAT MUST I DO?

And at midnight, Paul and סִילָא, Siyla were praying *and* singing praises to God, and the prisoners
were hearing them. Then, suddenly, a massive
earthquake came, so that the foundations of the
prison were shaken, and all the doors were instantly opened, and the bonds of all *the prisoners*
were loosened. And the jailer, having come out of
sleep and having seen the doors of the prison open,
having drawn the sword, was about to kill himself,
thinking the prisoners to have fled. But Paul called
out with a loud voice, saying, "You should not do
yourself any harm, for we are all here!" And having
asked for the lights, he sprang in; and trembling,
he fell down before Paul and סִילָא, Siyla and, having brought them out, said, "Sirs, what must I
do—that I may be saved?" –Acts 16:25-30

Paul, Siyla and Luke had arrived in Philippi, where Paul got
himself into trouble once again. After being severely beaten,
Paul and Siyla were thrown into prison, and the jailer there
was ordered to guard them securely. He placed them in the
most fortified area of the inner prison, and locked their feet in
the stocks. They weren't going anywhere.

That night, as the jailer slept, and as Paul and Siyla were praying
and singing praises to God, there was a massive earthquake,
and all the doors of the prison were instantly opened. When
the jailer awoke, he saw the opened doors, and, thinking all
the prisoners had escaped, drew his sword to kill himself. "But
Paul called out with a loud voice, saying, 'You should not do
yourself any harm, for we are all here!'" Trembling, the jailer

fell down before Paul and said, "What must I do—that I may be saved?"

Just like that.

Like the jailer, most everyone has an urgent or pressing need to be saved from something. Maybe it's related to health or finances or employment or relationships or any infinite number of things. In the jailer's case, he believed he was facing severe retribution for losing his prisoners. So the jailer's response to Paul was not because of the powerful demonstration in the earthquake—indeed, he slept right through it! No, he was ready to listen to Paul because Paul had just saved his life.

When you show that you care by reaching out to affect a person's life with personal, practical help, for all you know, you may literally be saving their life. A helpful hand will get some people's attention easier than an earthquake. Don't believe that you have nothing to offer another soul in need. Just determine to be selfless and helpful; then, when they are gratefully astonished with what you have done, be ready to tell them how to *truly* be saved.

PRAYER

Adonai, how can I help other people when I have worries and needs of my own? Can't I just pray for them, and then leave it all in Your hands? Forgive me, Abba, for my selfishness and fear—for failing to love my neighbor as much as I love myself. Convict my heart, Master, provoke me toward action, and remind me from where all true salvation comes...

THEY RECEIVED THE WORD

> And the brothers immediately, during the night, sent out to Berea both Paul and סִילָא, Siyla, who, having come, went to the synagogue of the יְהוּדִים, Y'hudiym. And these were more noble than those in Thessalonica, *for* they received the word with all readiness of mind, every day examining the Scriptures *to find out* whether those things were so. –ACTS 17:10-11

Paul and Siyla continued to move from city to city, entering into the synagogues of the Y'hudiym and reasoning with them from the Scriptures that Yeshua is the Messiah. When they came to Berea, the Y'hudiym there refreshingly "received the word with all readiness of mind, every day examining the Scriptures *to find out* whether those things [that Paul taught them] were so."

Today, most of us in the Body of Messiah don't think twice about what we're taught. If the teaching appeals to us on an emotional level, or makes us feel good about our walk with God, or alleges to reveal some kind of previously hidden mystery, we're all ears. For too many of us, the teacher could be quoting from the Bible or the Book of Mormon or the Koran and we wouldn't know the difference. It's not so much that we implicitly trust our teachers; it's that we are essentially unfamiliar with God's word, and often unmotivated to know it any more than superficially.

The Bereans were "noble" because they approached the Scriptures not in search of "nuggets" of truth, or supports for their pre-existing beliefs, or cliché out-of-context quotes, but with "readiness of mind" to learn the truth *for themselves*—and they did this, not when it was convenient, or when they felt they had the time or energy, but "every day."

As dedicated disciples of Messiah, we must not be lazy or casual with the Scriptures, simply absorbing and regurgitating whatever we hear from the pulpit or (worse!) the internet. Be responsible for your faith, and put forth the effort to examine the word *every day* for yourself. Your understanding will not be built simply by hearing it second-hand, but when you do the work yourself "to find out whether those things [you hear are] so."

PRAYER

ADONAI, make me as the Bereans, and implant in me a passion for the unimpeded, unfiltered truth of Your word. Give me a ready mind, God, to receive Your word and have it utterly change my mind. Thank You, Master, for Your good and righteous teachers, who do not impose their ideas and interpretations on Your word. I don't want to know You by hearsay, Yeshua! Send me to the Scriptures every day to examine them—to find and to know You more...

BOUND BY THE RUACH

"[L]ook! I—bound by the רוּחַ, Ruach—go on to יְרוּשָׁלַיִם, Y'rushalayim not knowing the things that will meet with me in it, except that the רוּחַ הַקֹּדֶשׁ, Ruach HaQodesh testifies fully to me in every city, saying that bonds and oppressions wait for me. But by no account do I make life precious to myself, so that I *will* finish my course and the service that I received from the Master יֵשׁוּעַ, Yeshua, to testify fully *of* the Good News of the *unmerited* favor of God. " –ACTS 20:22-24

The Feast of Shavuot was fast approaching. Paul had been traveling extensively for years, sharing the faith of Yeshua, leading many to believe—and making many enemies. Now he was hurrying to return to Y'rushalayim, hoping to make it in time for the Feast...

...but the Feast was not the only reason he was going.

As Paul explained to the z'qeniym of the Called-Forth community, he felt a compulsion and drive—a binding—by the Ruach to go on to Y'rushalayim, knowing yet not knowing the things that would meet him there. Essentially, he was telling them that he didn't have a choice, but was fully submitted to the Ruach. Though the breadth of his foreknowledge was unclear, the testimony of the Ruach HaQodesh within him was not: bonds and oppressions awaited Paul in Y'rushalayim. Still, he had to go.

Paul considered nothing—not even his own life—more precious than finishing the "course and the service that [he] received from the Master יֵשׁוּעַ, Yeshua." "To testify fully *of* the

Good News of the *unmerited* favor of God" *was* Paul's life. He had no life of his own—there was no other purpose to distract him or to mislead him or to consider of greater importance. Therefore, with an inkling of the difficulties ahead—although unable to see the end—he was still determined to see it through, remaining firmly in the bondage of the Ruach.

Do you feel compelled, driven and bound by the Ruach? Or are you unfocused and untethered—just drifting through life? If you are Messiah's, then the testimony of the Ruach is speaking deep within you today. It's time to listen, hear and obey—no matter the price. Finish your course and service to God; live not your own life, but one given completely over to Him… doing all that you are bound to do.

PRAYER

O God, I know You are speaking—please let me hear You in my innermost parts. Give me a clear, set purpose in life, Abba, that I may know and do my service for You. Cause Your Ruach to testify fully within me, Master, but even more than that, give me the courage and conviction to do as He says, "not knowing the things that will meet with me." Drive me and compel me, Ruach HaQodesh; make my life unprecious in my eyes, that I may finish my course, willingly bound by You.

ACCORDING TO THE WAY

> "But I confess this to you: that, according to the Way (which they call a sect), I so serve the God of the fathers, believing all things that have been written in the תּוֹרָה, Torah and in the Prophets...."
>
> –ACTS 24:14

Paul knew the dangers of returning to Y'rushalayim, and, as expected, he was soon apprehended by the Y'hudiym. After being transferred to Roman custody, he eventually came before the governor, Felix. The high priest's hired gun, Tertullus, proceeded to lead the attack of false accusations against Paul, trying to make a case to Felix. So Paul responded by opening his mouth and making a full confession.

Paul confessed that he was a servant of God—the God of the fathers of those who would see him imprisoned or dead. Paul confessed his belief in the writings of Scripture—the Torah and the prophets—as the source of his divine instructions for service. He confessed his "hope toward God" that this life was not the end, but that "there is about to be a Rising Again" from the dead (24:15). And he confessed that both the righteous and the unrighteous alike will rise—each one to his own fate. Doing his "best to have a conscience always void of offense toward God and men" (24:16), Paul confessed "the Way" before his oppressors—not simply in defense of himself, but for the salvation of their souls.

How many of us are prepared to make such a concise yet thorough confession of the Good News of God? And how many of us are willing to speak that uncompromised truth *before* we have nothing left to lose? Paul was blameless of the accusations against him, and was therefore confident of the moral ground upon which he stood. Can we say the same of our testimony, or is our compromised walk standing in the way of the Good News we are meant to proclaim?

What is your confession today? In words and in actions, show them the Way.

PRAYER

ADONAI, God of my fathers, make me worthy to serve You and confess Your Name before men! I *do* believe all the things that have been written in the Torah and the Prophets, and I have absolute hope toward You for the Rising Again from the dead. Bind my tongue, hands and feet, Master, that I may speak, do and go only according to Your word. Help me to not be offensive to You in my actions and to others in my words, but let them see the blamelessness of my testimony, and hear Your matchless truth in my confession.

THE JUDGMENT THAT IS COMING

> And after *a* certain *number of* days, Felix, having come with Drusilla his wife (*she* being יְהוּדִיָּה, Y'hudiyah), sent for Paul and heard him regarding the faith toward Messiah יֵשׁוּעַ, Yeshua. And he *was* reasoning about righteousness and self-control and the judgment that is coming. *And* Felix, having become afraid, answered, "Be going for now, and having gotten time, I will call for you...." –Acts 24:24-25

Having heard from both Paul and his accusers, Felix, the Roman governor of Y'hudah, decided to delay the rest of the hearing. After a number of days, Felix returned with his Jewish wife and sent for Paul in order for him to proceed with his testimony regarding the faith in the Messiah Yeshua. So Paul continued, and "was reasoning about righteousness and self-control and the judgment that is coming..."

"And Felix [became] afraid...."

Many people are unafraid of the "judgment that is coming" because it is unreal to them—they don't believe it. Indeed, why would anyone be afraid of anything that is either make-believe, or is something they can't even imagine? Yet Felix became afraid not simply because Paul described or warned him of the coming judgment, but because he first reasoned with him about righteousness and self-control—Paul showed Felix how his own actions and behavior would impact the way he would eventually be judged forever...

...and that thought should scare all of us.

As believers in Yeshua, too often we do not truly fear the judgment that is coming, and instead have an aversion to righteousness and self-control. We continue to allow our flesh and emotions to influence our thoughts and behavior. We don't remember—or don't believe—that our actions will affect our future.

How have your actions and attitudes been lately? How will *you* fare in the coming judgment?

In Messiah, there's no need to be afraid. Just make sure that—in the coming judgment—you won't be taken by surprise...

PRAYER

Father, search me today and reveal my heart to me. Show me, Abba, where I have been unrighteous and out of control, giving in to my flesh, emotions and selfishness. Help me, Master, to not fool myself into believing that I am secure, when I have clearly placed myself in danger through my own attitudes and behavior. Make Your judgment and salvation truly real to me, ADONAI. Teach me to see reason—to become afraid if I must—and then to put all my hope and trust in You...

JUDGED INCREDIBLE

> "Why is it judged incredible with you *all* if God raises the dead?" –Acts 26:8

After two years of imprisonment under the governor Felix, Paul was eventually brought before Agrippa, the Judean king. Being permitted to speak, Paul proceeded to once again make a defense for himself, in the course of which he asked his Jewish audience the singular question at the heart of both their curiosity and contempt: "Why is it judged incredible with you *all* if God raises the dead?"

To everyone who has ever professed belief in the God of Israel, Paul's question addresses the very core of that faith. What could possibly be judged too incredible for God to accomplish? Is giving life back to one who is dead truly out of God's reach?

When we ask ourselves to consider what might be too incredible for God, we are forced to make choices about what we actually believe to be true. If God is limited in what He can do—if He is unable to accomplish the impossible—then what kind of god is He really? And what does that say of our faith in Him? What good is such a faith?

But what if God is able to do *anything* He wants—*especially* the impossible, the unscientific, the unbelievable? *Then* what kind of God is He? And what kind of believers are *we*? If we accept that nothing can be judged too incredible for this God, then we are forced to accept that He can come dwell with us as a man who lived a sinless life and died for our sins, and that He raised that man from the dead. But even more than that, when we believe that this God is endlessly incredible, we have no choice but to submit to His will, and to believe and to do according to every word He says.

Trust completely in ADONAI today, and believe Him for *everything*. Indeed, what is too incredible for your God to do?

PRAYER

ADONAI, God of Israel, nothing is too incredible for You! All creation hears Your command, and obeys. Who am I, God, to not only doubt Your word, but to doubt that You can do anything You choose? Teach me, Father, to not put limits on Your will or abilities, but to have a limitless faith in You. I praise You, Master, and Your unsearchable ways—O my God, You are incredible!

MESSIAH-FOLLOWER

> [And Paul said,] "King Agrippa, do you believe the prophets? I have known that you do believe!" And Agrippa said to Paul, "In a little *time* you *will* persuade me, to make *me* a 'Messiah-follower'!" And Paul said, "I would have prayed to God—both in a little *time* and in much—not only *for* you, but also *for* all those hearing me today, to become such as I also am, except *for* these bonds." –Acts 26:27-29

Paul continued to testify before the Judean king Agrippa. He spoke of his successful campaign to persecute and imprison Jewish believers in Yeshua. He recounted his dramatic, life-altering encounter with the risen Yeshua. And he told of the persecution he himself faced from his own people for turning toward Israel's Messiah and being obedient to God. When Paul reiterated how Yeshua fulfills Mosheh and the prophets—reminding Agrippa of what he already believed to be true—Agrippa interrupted and exclaimed, "In a little *time* you *will* persuade me, to make *me* a 'Messiah-follower'!" One way or another, Agrippa's spirit had begun to stir.

Was King Agrippa speaking ironically, suggesting that Paul was mistaken if he thought a few minutes of testimony would be sufficient to cause him to believe? Or was he truly taken aback, realizing that the power and truth of Paul's words were piercing his heart and kindling his very soul? Either way, one thing is clear: Paul had awakened within Agrippa an awareness that what he was hearing had potentially existential ramifications, and it was almost too much to bear.

The truth of the Scriptures, coupled with authentic personal testimony, will do nothing but work powerfully in the heart and mind of those willing to hear. Our responsibility, then, is to be completely committed to God, to fully know His word, to be spiritually discerning of those with whom we are sharing Yeshua, and to be ready at all times to boldly declare what we believe—to proclaim only what the Scriptures say.

Are you ready to make Messiah-followers? Are you prepared to persuade?

PRAYER

Father, I know that my testimony doesn't compare to Paul's, yet at one time, I was Your enemy too. Help me to see the value in whatever testimony is mine, and to be convicted that it is worthy to share. I praise You, ADONAI, for the truth of Your word, and its power to persuade the hearts and minds of men. Thank You, Abba, for calling me as a Messiah-follower—now persuade *me* to make more Messiah-followers for You.

BELIEVE GOD
THAT IT WILL BE SO

> "Therefore, take courage, men! For I believe God
> that it will be so, even as it has been spoken to me."
> —ACTS 27:25

King Agrippa had determined Paul's innocence; nevertheless, Paul remained in custody, bound for Rome—bound for
Cæsar. Having set sail for Italy, after many days the Ruach
HaQodesh gave Paul knowledge that his ship would soon
be in peril. Though he admonished the crew to stay in safe
harbor rather than pressing on, his warning regrettably went
unheeded, and they quickly encountered a tempestuous wind
and increasingly dangerous weather. Storm-tossed and sailing
blindly, "all the hope of [their] being saved was finally taken
away" (27:20).

Paul, then, standing in the middle of them, began to exhort
and encourage the men. He testified that a Messenger of God
had appeared to him, telling him not to be afraid, and he
assured them that despite the hurt and damage and danger,
not one of them would lose their lives. Paul had heard the
voice of God, and he "believe[d] God that it will be so, even
as it has been spoken to me."

We too, like the men on Paul's ship, rarely heed godly warnings. Indeed, we are more likely to be set in our ways, keeping
our own counsel. We charge ahead with our plans, judging
the future based solely on the present, deaf to the voice of
the Ruach that is speaking within us. And inevitably we find
ourselves caught in the storm, wondering where we went
wrong...

And yet, He continues to speak.

In the middle of the storm—hurt, in danger, tossed about and blind, with all hope having been taken away—will you still listen for the voice of God? Submit to His authority at all times and believe what He says will be so...

...perhaps you may even avoid the storm.

PRAYER

O Father, when will I learn? How many calamities must I endure before I choose to heed Your warnings? Send me Your Ruach, ADONAI, that I may know Your plans and, most importantly, finally listen. Speak to me, God, and I will believe! Grant me the courage, Master, to brave every storm.

BECAUSE OF THE HOPE

> "For this reason, therefore, I called for you, to see
> and to speak with you, for because of the hope
> of יִשְׂרָאֵל, Yis'rael, with this chain I am bound."
> —ACTS 28:20

Following years of imprisonment, Paul was finally delivered
to Rome to await his appearance before Cæsar. After several
days he called together the Jewish leaders, declaring that while
his present predicament was the result of persecution by his
own people, it was "because of the hope of יִשְׂרָאֵל, Yis'rael [that]
with this chain I am bound." Not only had Paul not been
working against Israel's interests, he had been laboring—even
suffering—for her salvation.

It's easy to forget why Paul endured such hardship. We ex-
tract him from his context, and see his adversity simply as the
result of proclaiming the truth, concluding only that truth
in and of itself invites persecution. But this valid perspective also causes us to lose sight of those for whom Paul was
ultimately fighting... even as he proclaimed Messiah among
the Gentiles. Everything Paul did had the salvation of his
own Jewish people at its end.

Paul proceeded to expound upon, testify to and persuade his
brothers that Yeshua was the Messiah, the hope of Yis'rael.
"And some, indeed, were believing the things spoken, and
some were not believing" (28:24). But no matter how many
eyes were closed and how many hearts were thick, Paul—the
emissary to the *Gentiles*—refused to stop declaring God's
word, believing that, one day, all *Israel* would be saved (Romans 11:26).

May it never be that we, as followers of the Jewish Messiah, neglect to expound upon, testify to, and persuade the Jewish people that Yeshua is Israel's one true hope. Let us not forget Paul's suffering, and be willing—for the sake of Yeshua's brothers—to endure the same.

PRAYER

O Adonai, Your Jewish people hear but do not understand—they see but will not perceive. Their ears are heavy and their hearts are thick—please turn them back to You and heal them! Drive me to Your word, Father, that I too may see and hear, so that I am not constantly presenting a "Yeshua" based on who man's religions have made Him to be. Teach my heart, Abba, to be willing to endure chains for the sake of Your word—and to face suffering for the hope of Yis'rael.

QUICKLY TRANSFERRED

> I *am in* wonder that you are so quickly transferred
> from Him who called you in the *unmerited* favor
> of Messiah, to another Good News (which is not
> *really* another), except *that* there are certain *ones*
> who are troubling you and *are* wanting to pervert
> the Good News of the Messiah. –GALATIANS 1:6-7

We sit in the pews and listen. We stand at our seats and
praise. We consume instruction from books and videos from
teachers who have never seen our face. We hear the word...
or some version of it; we read it for ourselves... maybe. We're
told what to believe, and we surrender our minds to those
ideas. It all appears to be correct and righteous and good...

But is it actually "another Good News"?

Since our Master walked the earth, there has only ever been
one Good News—one message of hope, one truth, one gate to
salvation. Yet also from the beginning there have always been
counter currents, deviations, perversions and misinformation.
Some of these would arise from well-meaning and zealous
but misguided teachers, permitting their thoughts to explore
God's will without bounds. Others would arise in an effort
to take advantage, grab power, exert influence and assume
authority...

And the sheep would follow the shepherds without question.

Are you thinking for yourself today? Or have you stopped
thinking? Are you just grazing along with the rest of the flock?
Or are you feeding directly from the word? Be careful! You
may have been "transferred from Him who called you" and

accepted "another Good News." Make sure that the Good News you live is not different than what you received from the Scriptures. Make sure you are influenced only by the one, true Word.

PRAYER

Father, when I read Your word, help me to not be "quickly transferred" from it to any version other than the truth. Teach me, Abba, to discern not just men's motives, but whether what they teach and practice is fully according to Your word. I praise You, Master, for Your Good News—for calling me in Your unmerited favor. Thank You, Yeshua, for shepherding me in Your flock, and for protecting me from every other "Good News."

I NO LONGER LIVE

> With Messiah I have been crucified, and I no longer live—but Messiah lives in me. And that which I now live in the flesh, I live in the faith of the Son of God, who loved me and gave Himself for me.
>
> —GALATIANS 2:19C-20

When we honestly come before Yeshua, it is with hope—hope that He can help us, change us... save us. In return, we gladly offer Him our allegiance and devotion—we are willing and happy to serve.

But then, He makes a demand we do not quite understand; He sets a condition that we neither expect nor desire. Our heart is yearning, yet our flesh resists, and we withdraw our hand ever so slightly from the salvation we seek.

It is in this moment that we realize that life in Messiah is deeper—and *harder*—than we were led to believe. No, *living* for Messiah means *dying*...

...to self.

Oh, we tell ourselves that it's figurative or poetic—that being crucified with Messiah is something we can never do, and nothing Yeshua would ever actually ask of us. But denying spiritual reality doesn't make the requirement any less true: before Messiah can live in you, you—the old you—must no longer live.

Yeshua gave Himself for you because He loved you and wants you to be alive forever. But the life He has for you today necessitates Him taking up permanent residence within you, and

He is unwilling to inhabit that space as long as you continue to occupy it.

Your wants, your hopes, your dreams, your needs—everything you think and know and *are* must be thrown down, never to be built up again. Let the Master recreate you—alive in the body, yet resurrected a new creation. For you are no longer *you*... but Messiah's.

PRAYER

O Yeshua, my Savior, with You, my old inner self has been truly crucified, and I no longer live. I am throwing myself down today; as I vacate the premises, come and live in me, so that I may "live to God." Let me not make void Your un-merited favor, Abba, causing the sacrifice of Your Son to be worth nothing. Help me now, Master, to fully live... as I die daily for You.

SO UNTHINKING!

> O unthinking Galatians! Who bewitched you—
> before whose eyes יֵשׁוּעַ, Yeshua *the* Messiah was
> previously described *as* crucified? I only want to
> learn this from you: did you receive the רוּחַ, Ru-
> ach by actions of תּוֹרָה, Torah, or by the hearing
> of faith? You are so unthinking! Having begun
> in the רוּחַ, Ruach, do you now finish in the flesh?
> —GALATIANS 3:1-3

"The תּוֹרָה, Torah, then: *is it* against the promises of God? Let
it not be!" (3:21). Yet, we often make it so, depending upon
our actions.

Sometimes, we see the Torah—neglected in the Body, absent
from our lives—and we approach it with curiosity, reverence
and love. It is foreign, yet familiar, and we peer inside to find
God embracing and being a father to His children. It stirs in
us the desire to obey...

...and sometimes, we shed our faith to enter.

What first drew us to the Torah—our love for the Messiah—
is set aside, as we enter what feels like a new world... a new
dimension of our faith. But soon, without even noticing, as
we behold the righteousness of God and long to reflect it in
ourselves, we begin to strive for that righteousness in a way
other than God intended—by taking off the *Messiah* and putting on the *Torah*.

And as we wrap ourselves in its commands, we begin to "do"
what the Torah says. And the more we do, the more righteous
we see ourselves, until we start to believe (though we would

never admit it) we have found a manageable means by which to *control God*—to rule how He perceives us and, thus, gain His approval.

And what began in the Ruach is finished in the flesh.

The Torah that is based on actions—a quid pro quo for God's righteousness in exchange for our obedience—is not of faith. It is a perversion of the good and holy Torah. It does not lead us back to the Messiah, but puts us under a curse.

No matter how much Torah we keep (or look like we're keeping by doing man's traditions instead), "by תּוֹרָה, Torah, no one is declared righteous before God" (3:11). So do the Torah, yes... but "live by faith" (3:11), for righteousness has been credited to you. Having begun in the flesh, now finish it in the Ruach.

PRAYER

ADONAI my God, forgive me for mistaking my fixation on the Torah with having faith in and following You. Teach me to understand the good and lawful use of Your Torah, and to know how to differentiate it from the legalism in my heart and actions. Cover me in Your righteousness, Father; clothe me in Your Son! Help me to not be "unthinking," but to remember the eternal work You are finishing in me.

CARRY THE BURDENS

> Brothers, if a man is also overtaken by any mis-
> step, you who *ARE* spiritual *should* restore such a
> one in a רוּחַ, ruach of humility, paying attention
> to yourself; otherwise, you also may be tempted.
> Carry the burdens of one another, and in this
> way you will fill up the תּוֹרָה, Torah of the Mes-
> siah... –GALATIANS 6:1-2

Is "carry[ing] the burdens of one another" really what we think
it is? When we stop to consider what it actually means (if we
pay attention to such an exhortation at all), we often marry
it with similar Scriptural instructions in the vein of meeting
physical and material needs. It's humanitarian in nature, or so
we believe. But while there is a time and a place for practical
benevolence, there is a certain kind of burden-carrying that
most of us would go to great lengths to avoid.

When we see a brother or sister falling into sin or struggling
with something spiritual, most of us tend to not want to meddle. Intervention leads to intrusion, intrusion to confrontation,
and confrontation to discomfort. And that's the best case sce-
nario. What we truly fear, however, is that our intrusion might
be welcomed, our confrontation heeded, and suddenly we
would find ourselves *being needed*—hence, *inconvenienced*.

Yet this is what it means to "carry the burdens of one another":
that when your brother or sister in the Messiah is "overtaken
by any misstep, you who *ARE* spiritual *should* restore such a
one." You are to learn of their struggles, walk with them as
they strive to overcome and succeed, and—most loathsome of

all—allow them abundant *time* and *access* to you. Only in this way can you truly help them in their restoration.

As Messiah-followers, we need to be there for each other. Don't let inconvenience and conceit inform either your compassion or your calendar, "think[ing yourself] to be something" (6:3) and making yourself unavailable to your fellow-believer. Reach out to your brother or sister in Messiah. Be willing to help carry those spiritual burdens, "and in this way you will fill up the תּוֹרָה, Torah of the Messiah."

PRAYER

Master Yeshua, thank You for showing me that my reluctance to reach out has not been about others, but about myself. Help me in my conceit, God, and humble me. Teach my heart, Abba, to be a burden-bearer—to be willing to give of myself freely and without trepidation—for the sake of restoring others. I praise You, ADONAI, for Your compassion and patience... and for never holding back either Your time or Your access from me.

OUR HOPE AND JOY

> Therefore, we wanted to come to you [brothers] (I, indeed—Paul), both once and again, but הַשָּׂטָן, Ha-Satan hindered us. For what *is* our hope or joy or crown of boasting? Is *it* not even you, in front of our Master יֵשׁוּעַ, Yeshua at His *coming* presence? For you are our glory and joy. –1 Thessalonians 2:18-20

When we approach the Scriptures or we go to God in prayer, it is usually for our comforting and edification. Our desire is to live a life pleasing to God, as we await our eternal life with Him and attempt to victoriously navigate the remainder of our days here on earth. We look to God for our hope and joy, and we gladly glorify Him in return.

All of this is good and right. It is a pattern of behavior that should not cease. It is an attitude we must hold onto and strengthen.

Nevertheless...

"For what *is* our hope or joy or crown of boasting? Is *it* not even you, in front of our Master יֵשׁוּעַ, Yeshua at His *coming* presence? For you are our glory and joy."

As we are looking to God and being uplifted by His word—receiving His gift of life age-enduring—at the same time, we are also supposed to be retransmitting what we learn and who we are becoming. We are to be passing it on to "you"—that is, to others. In this case, then, our hope and joy and glory does not come by way of a direct connection to God, but rather by completing the circuit as we channel our devotion to God through the making of our own *disciples*.

When the Master returns, He will not be pleased with us simply because we prayed and sought Him and looked to improve our lives by living according to His word. Rather, we will multiply His pleasure with us according to how we multiplied ourselves—by making new devoted followers for Him.

What is your hope or joy or crown of boasting? Impart the Messiah in you to others, and dedicate yourself to multiplying disciples for Yeshua. Then be ever more glorified in front of the Master Himself when He returns at His glorious and coming presence.

PRAYER

Master Yeshua, help me to see beyond myself and truly perceive the eternal impact of my inaction. ADONAI, give me disciples, that I may pour out into them the glory that I have in You. Teach me, Father, of the hope and joy that generous discipleship multiplies in Your sight. I seek Your face, and I desire to be pleasing before You, Abba. Come soon, Master Yeshua, and be abundantly pleased with me.

A QUIET LIFE

> But we call upon you... to abound still more, and *also* to make it your aim to live a quiet life, and to tend to your own *things*, and to work with your own hands (as we commanded you), so that you may walk respectably toward those outside, and may have lack of nothing. –1 Thessalonians 4:10B-12

What comes to mind—what do we pursue—when we think about "experiencing God?" Every week, we gather together expecting dynamic praise and worship, a powerful message from the word, and the palpable presence of God. Or we head to the city street corner with our bullhorn and Bible, hoping for curious onlookers, colorful debate and seeking souls. Or we venture out to the mission field, forgoing familiar comforts, adopting the primitive, and suffering for the sake of the Good News. This is what living for God is truly all about. Anything less is just not enough.

Clearly, we have the wrong idea.

For some reason, we have the stereotypical impression that living for Messiah ought to mean excitement and thrilling experiences. We think that in order to feel alive for God, we must maintain a certain level of adventure and intensity... and if we're not, there's something wrong with our walk. Without a doubt, there are times and places when God causes His people to intersect with unusual, authentic experiences. But these are not the norm, and we aren't supposed to contrive the feelings associated with such events, hoping that they are real.

Rather, for most of us, most of the time, we are supposed to "aim to live a quiet life"—a life where God, ministry and discipleship are all experienced as a matter of course; a life where, instead of in intense episodes, we experience God naturally and continually; a life where sharing and encountering God is integrated into the fabric of our lives—everywhere we go, with whomever we meet.

God is not in the experience... the experience is in God's presence in our normal, everyday lives. Don't seek extraordinary excitement or exhilarating weekly events in order to feel alive in God. Live quietly; do the steady, simple work of God daily; and, surely, you "may have lack of nothing."

PRAYER

ADONAI, thank You for choosing me to serve You and dedicate my life wholly to You. Teach me Your ways, God, that You may work powerfully through me even in my boring, regular life. Help me to see You, Master, not in the stage lights and spectacle, but in the holy use of my hands and feet. Thank You, Yeshua, for raising my valleys and lowering my mountains; thank You for giving me a quiet life.

WE ARE NOT OF DARKNESS

> [F]or you are all sons of light and sons of day. We are not of night nor of darkness. So, then, we should not sleep as the others, but *stay* awake and be sober. –1 THESSALONIANS 5:5-6

When the Master returns, it will be as a thief in the night: few will be ready, but many, unprepared—blind in the dark and caught utterly by surprise.

Some will be found asleep in their activity—just keeping busy, and running the rat race; or perhaps engaging in their resistance, disruption, fighting and fighting back.

Others will be asleep in their isolation—some huddled in their homes, keeping to themselves; some shrouding their eyes and covering their ears, trying to shut out the vitriol, contentiousness, insanity and noise.

Others still will be asleep in their ignorance—wandering, aimless, oblivious, and hopeless.

The world is "of night [and] darkness." Whether that darkness is shade, shadow or black as pitch, the world is drunk on time and air—living and breathing, yet unaware that soon life and breath will give way. They walk forever in a waking slumber, unconscious to their living death.

Yet we, the followers of the Messiah Yeshua, are "sons of light [and] day." As such, we must not rest, but work diligently and be committed to "not sleep as the others, but *stay* awake and be sober." While those in darkness shrink from the light, we who are in the light must resist the lure of that darkness. We must remain vigilant as we call into the dark, trying to wake as many as we can.

Be sober, then. Have faith, love and a hope of salvation, for God did not appoint you for wrath. The Day is coming, and the whole world is asleep... have you been slumbering with them?

PRAYER

Father, I am so drowsy; my eyes have grown heavy from the relentless lullaby of the world. Help me to remain awake, Master—to not be lulled asleep either by the droning of life or the dreaminess of sin. Come quickly, Master Yeshua! I eagerly await Your Day! Teach me, God, to yearn for Your light and to shun the darkness of the world. Let me be awake and alert when Your Son suddenly returns.

SAY THE SAME THING

> And I call upon you, brothers, through the Name
> of our Master יֵשׁוּעַ, Yeshua *the* Messiah, that you
> all say the same thing, and there may not be di-
> visions among you, and you may be perfectly unit-
> ed in the same mind and in the same judgment.
>
> –1 CORINTHIANS 1:10

From "Messianics" to "Christians" to everything in between,
we all have our own opinions and interpretations of Scripture.
Yes, we generally adhere to certain concepts and doctrines
within our distinct faith traditions, but when we come up
against something that rubs us the wrong way or challenges
our point of view, we fight it or change it or ignore it as we
deem fit. Eventually—if we receive enough resistance, or just
feel sufficiently unwelcome—we simply divide and separate,
and then huddle together with others who also think the same
"new" way that we do… at least, for now.

But how many interpretations of Scripture can be right? How
many ways of looking at the same passage can be different—
even in direct conflict with one another—yet be correct?

Only one way: MINE.

Or yours. Or *neither*.

Because we can't both be right. We actually, literally, cannot
both be right.

When we disagree on what the Scripture says, there should
be no such thing as agreeing to disagree. There should be no
holding to different points of view. If we are truly members

of the same Body, then we must not *divide*, but *unite*—we must "say the same thing," have the "same mind," and share the "same judgment." Where it comes to understanding and walking out the Scriptures, diversity of thought is a plague. We are granted no freedom in Messiah to think differently from one another with regard to God's word...

...and when we do, the Scriptures *alone* must be our arbiter.

When you're in disagreement over what the word says, remember that every Scripture has *only one meaning*, and we are beholden to find that meaning—together. If we will commit to investigating that glorious, spiritual, wonderful document *without preconceptions*, we *will* reach the exact same conclusion.

You are not entitled to your own understanding of Scripture, so don't continue to participate in the dismemberment of Messiah's Body. Instead, take every opportunity to be "the same" with your brother, and become "perfectly united" in word and mind.

PRAYER

Master Yeshua, You are not divided; convict my heart to not be a separator of Your people. Show me, Abba, the foolishness of my wisdom, and the haughtiness of my mind. Help me, Father, to be a seeker of unity by championing the perfection of Your word over my own reasonings. Teach me, ADONAI, to put away my sense of entitlement to my own opinions, and to be willing to work through the word with others, so that we may all think as one—convinced solely by the Scriptures, and saying only the same thing.

FOOLISH THINGS

> [B]ut to those *who are* called (both יְהוּדִים, Y'hudiym and Greeks), Messiah *is* the power of God and the wisdom of God, because the foolishness of God is wiser than men, and the weakness of God is stronger than men. For see your calling, brothers: that not many *ARE* wise according to the flesh; not many *are* mighty; not many *are* noble. But God chose the foolish things of the world so that He might put the wise to shame; and God chose the weak things of the world so that He might put the strong to shame. –I CORINTHIANS I:24-27

When you were called by Messiah, He did something in you much greater than you realize. God saw all the wise and powerful people in the world, and He knew that if there was ever any hope of reaching them, He would first have to confound their wisdom and weaken their strength. So since "the foolishness of God is wiser than men, and the weakness of God is stronger than men", God needed to find a way for the noble and mighty ones of the earth to observe His weakness and foolishness…

…so He chose you.

Yes, God took one look at you and decided that you were just the right amount of feeble and dense to be of some use to Him. It was irrelevant that you would either think too highly of yourself or believe yourself unworthy of Him, because what He saw was the perfect balance of conceit and stupidity.

And that's when God decided to do this great thing in you— something far greater than anyone ever deserved. He took dumb, arrogant, flimsy and fragile you, and gave you both "the power of God and the wisdom of God"—He gave you to the Messiah.

God has chosen the foolish and weak things of the world to put the wise and strong to shame. God, therefore, has chosen *you*—the weakest and most foolish vessel He could find—so that the world would see *His* wisdom and strength. In Messiah, you fulfill your purpose as a "thing[ ] that [is] not, so that He might make useless the things that are" (1:28). In you, He truly made something out of nothing.

So boast not before God, but find humility and comfort in your foolishness and weaknesses. For this is the way you were called by God, so that He could remake and use you for His purposes... a weakling and a fool for Messiah.

PRAYER

Oh Yeshua, I am an idiot. No matter how strong or wise I perceive myself, I am nothing in the shadow of Your wisdom and strength. Let me feel neither pride nor shame about who I am, ADONAI, but instead remember that it is Yeshua in me who can confound the noble and mighty. Use me, God—a thing that is not—to make useless the things that are. I boast in You, Master, my strength and wisdom; thank You for choosing a weak and foolish thing like me.

HIDDEN THINGS

> So then, judge nothing before the time, until the Master comes, who will both bring to light the hidden things of the darkness, and reveal the purposes of the hearts. And then the praise will come to each *one* from God. –1 CORINTHIANS 4:5

It is lurking there, underneath. It has been dormant, perhaps for what seems like ages. That was another life, another time, and you've all but forgotten who that person was—or so you tell yourself. And yet, you sometimes catch a fleeting glimpse of honesty in the mirror, and hear the alluring voice in your head, whispering. There's something familiar stirring, swimming around in the dark. And before you know it, it has you again.

When the Master Yeshua purchased you with His precious blood, He knew the treasure He had obtained, though it was yet wrapped in a stinking sack of flesh. He knew the struggles you would endure in your striving to overcome a former way of life—the attempt to separate your eternal existence from the temporary one in which you still abide.

And so we remain susceptible—inclined to give way when the lurker regains his foothold. Yes, we walk with our eyes fixed on the author of faith, having the mind of Messiah and embracing our new reality in Him. But though the spirit is fully renewed, the flesh is merely biding its time, waiting for a moment of weakness it can exploit... if we will just allow it.

When the Master comes, He will "both bring to light the hidden things of the darkness and reveal the purposes of the heart." It is not inevitable that we will even briefly return to our fleshly, sinful past. Nevertheless, we need to be honest with ourselves about how virile and close to the surface those old ways still really are. We must remain ever vigilant, yet without fear or self-condemnation.

So be ashamed when you temporarily go insane and forget who you are in Messiah. But then, welcome the revealing light of Yeshua, and turn your heart back toward Salvation again…

"…and then the praise will come to each *one* from God."

PRAYER

Father, my flesh stinks! No matter how clean I look and behave outwardly, let me never forget how I must continually yield to You within. ADONAI, bring out into the light everything I keep hidden in the darkness, that I may not become lost in my self-deception. Reveal to me, God, the purposes of my heart, so I may know my true intentions toward You. Judge me, Master, for I am at Your mercy; I hope for and rely upon Your humbling praise…

IF I DO THIS WILLINGLY

> For if I proclaim Good News, it is no boasting for me, for obligation is laid upon me, for אוֹי, oy! *it* is to me if I do not proclaim *the* Good News. For if I do this willingly, I have a reward; but if unwillingly, I have *nevertheless* been entrusted with a stewardship! –1 CORINTHIANS 9:16-17

A certain amount of what Paul wrote was in defense of his work as an emissary. He was trying to communicate his commitment both to his readers and to God, and to provide evidence for why anyone would listen to him and heed his words.

Paul speaks here of the *obligation* he is under to proclaim Good News: if he does not proclaim it, it is "אוֹי, oy!" to him— meaning that he would have to face weighty consequences from God if it went neglected. He also admits that he has only two choices with regard to fulfilling that obligation: he can do it willingly, or unwillingly. If he does it willingly, he has a reward, and God will be pleased with him; but if he does it unwillingly, his attitude does not release him from his obligation. Either way, he has been "entrusted with a stewardship."

So Paul, as an anointed emissary, had an obligation from and to God, and he had a choice whether to fulfill that obligation willingly or unwillingly. But what about the rest of us? We are not all emissaries—and, certainly, none of us are Paul. So the question is: do we also have that obligation to proclaim Yeshua?

If we are not duty-bound to share the Good News with others, then what honest justification can we offer for hoarding the salvation we've received? Is the accepting of Yeshua supposed to be a non-repeatable, dead-end event within us that we never duplicate in others? Is the Good News supposed to set us free from all obligations, rather than obligate us to God's service?

Obligation is a bad word only to those who don't like being told what to do, or having anything expected of them. Rather, we would all do well to willingly accept any obligation that our Savior God places upon us. Let us not fool ourselves and think that sharing the Good News should flow simply from feelings of love and does not require an obligation to compel us. Indeed, refusing to meet our obligations doesn't make us any less obliged... it only makes us unwilling.

PRAYER

ADONAI, I may not be Your anointed emissary, but surely I am Your slave! You bought me at a price, Yeshua, and now I am Yours—obligated to You, whether I act like I am or not. Teach me, Master, to be willing to do all that You expect of me, especially the generous proclamation of the Good News. I hope for my reward, and freely receive Your salvation; I accept every obligation that comes with it, O God... now lay it on me.

LET NO ONE SEEK HIS OWN

> "All things are permitted," but not all things are profitable. "All things are permitted," but not all things build up. Let no one seek his own, but *one* another's. –1 CORINTHIANS 10:23-24

How does one live a completely unselfish life? How do you walk through the day not considering yourself and looking out for your own interests? If we aren't motivated to meet our own needs, what would even get us out of bed every morning? Is it even possible to wake up every day thinking only of the needs of others?

This is one of the most mind-blowing and seemingly impossible commands of Scripture: "Let no one seek his own, but *one* another's." How do you even begin to parse such a concept? Surely it can't be absolute. There just has to be some wiggle room in there somewhere. Maybe it's applied only in certain circumstances! What does a life like this even look like?

And here is where we realize the problem. If all I'm doing is looking out for others, then who is looking out for me? How can I trust other people to do the same for me?

Thus, we find the entire point of the command: It's not about putting your trust in others. It's about counting on God.

The command isn't telling you to never consider your own needs; it's encouraging you to trust *ADONAI* to take care of you, and instead use your strength and resources to take care of others rather than yourself. It's about putting the needs of others above your own—sacrificially—just as the Master Yeshua did for you.

Don't worry about losing yourself and going without as you seek to meet the needs of others. You can always be selfless just a little bit more—that is, if you want only to be like Yeshua.

PRAYER

Master Yeshua, how did You live so selflessly and sacrificially? How did You put the needs of the whole world above Your own? You are my example, Master; I heed Your command to deny myself and follow You. Teach me how to put the needs of others above my own all day long. But more than that, Abba, teach me to trust You, that I will not hoard myself in the hopes of simply providing for my own things. I praise You ADONAI, my Savior; help me to find You in the building-up of others.

THE LOVE NEVER FAILS

> The love is patient; it is kind. The love does not envy; it does not boast *of* itself. *It* is not puffed up, does not act unbecomingly, does not seek its own things, is not provoked, does not *keep* count *of* wrong, rejoices not over the unrighteousness, but rejoices with the truth. It bears all things; it believes all things; it hopes all things; it endures all things. The love never fails... –1 CORINTHIANS 13:4-8A

One of the most profound and sublime passages of Scripture is so objectively magnificent, breathtaking and true that even unbelievers read it at their weddings and hang it on the walls of their homes. It serves as a divine reminder for newlyweds and married couples alike of how they should act outwardly toward one another as an expression of their deep, inward and abiding love.

Not to take away from the weight and beauty of these timeless pronouncements, we would nevertheless be in great error if we only considered them in this secondary context. Indeed, when these words were initially penned, their author was not offering marital advice or making general observations about love. Not at all. On the contrary, these words were originally intended as *correction* for the whole Body of Messiah—an exposition of the "far *more* excellent way" (12:31) toward *unity*.

Though spiritual gifts may abound for the "common good" (12:7) of the Body's members, they are of no consequence, no meaning and no benefit without a patient, kind, unenvious and unboastful love—the kind of love that builds up the Body of Messiah, causes us to put away childish thinking, and puts the practice and purpose of things such as spiritual gifts in their proper place: all for the selfless sake of others. Love— true love—restores our focus to where it rightfully belongs. Love never allows us to put our own things first.

A dismembered Body that is toying with spiritual novelties or neglecting its common good will produce only further dismemberment. Instead, in the context of our disagreements as sincere believers, let us not focus on ourselves, our aims or our hurts, but turn our hearts toward love... the hopeful, enduring, and unifying kind.

PRAYER

Abba, I receive Your correction and admonishment; help me to make useless the childish things. Show me Your ways, ADONAI, that I may not seek Your spiritual things with wrong and unloving motives. I praise Your Name, Yeshua; let me know and see You fully, as I put the up-building of Your Body before myself. Teach me, Father, of Your far more excellent way—the way of unity that comes only through unfailing love.

BE NOT LED ASTRAY

> Be not led astray: "Evil associations corrupt good character." Wake up *from your stupor*, as is right, and sin not; for certain *ones* have an ignorance of God (I say *THIS* to you for shame). – 1 CORINTHIANS 15:33-34

Many believers—especially among the younger generations—maintain two separate social spheres. One is within the community of believers, and one is not. We have people with whom we share our worship, and people with whom we share our time... and never the twain shall meet.

Sometimes these divisions are thrust upon us, as in the case of an unbelieving spouse. But more often, we have simply grown accustomed to the relationship dynamics in our life, and we see no need for change. So we maintain relationships with unbelievers, not in the hopes of bringing them to Messiah, but because we are used to their company and the things we do together. Though we ought to be actively sharing our faith with them, rather than simply engaging on a superficial, worldly or emotional level, we are instead perpetuating our own dichotomy—and losing our true selves, bit by bit, every day.

We love our unsaved family and friends and are committed to them—often more deeply than we are committed to members of the Body of Messiah. Yet we cannot escape the reality that "evil associations corrupt good character." When we *passively* spend our time with unbelievers, it is we—not our family and friends—who will slowly bear the moral and spiritual consequences.

If this is you, and you do not find a way to bring the two halves of your life together, one side will suffer—and most likely, it will be the Messiah's side. Find a way to either share your faith *actively* and *often* with your unsaved family and friends, or—outside of an unequally yoked marriage—begin lessening those relationships, and start cultivating believing ones, not just for your own sake, but for the sake of Messiah.

"Wake up *from your stupor*, as is right, and sin not." How is your character being corrupted today?

PRAYER

Father, let me not be led astray. Awaken me to the reality of my relationships, and show me what I need to do to change. Strengthen my character, ADONAI; help me to admit the evil associations I maintain, and to stop believing that I am unaffected by them. Show me, Master, how I have perpetrated the false dichotomy of separating the people with whom I pray and worship from the people with whom I spend my time. Bring all the parts of my life together, God, and make me an active witness. Give me the courage and wisdom to make associations only for the glory of Your Name.

A MOST EXCELLENT TREASURE

> But we have this treasure in earthen containers, so
> that the excellency of the power is of God, and not
> of us: being pressed on every side, but not com-
> pressed; perplexed, but not in despair; persecuted,
> but not abandoned; struck down, but not destroyed;
> at all times carrying around in the body the dying
> of יֵשׁוּעַ, Yeshua, so that the life of יֵשׁוּעַ, Yeshua may
> also be revealed in our body. – 2 CORINTHIANS 4:7-10

Is what God gives us enough? It is a question that at once is
completely self-absorbed, yet also desperate. Too often it feels
as if we are struggling to reach the next rung, striving to take
the next step, fighting to make the next end meet. And not
only does it seem deeply overwhelming, but it's as if we are
receiving no heavenly assistance at all. "God! Where are You?
Do You not hear me? Am I not pleasing to You? Please! Help
me!"

Yet it is in our suffering—indeed, one day, in the coming oppression and persecution for the Name of Yeshua—that we
may glorify God. For "we have this treasure in earthen con-
tainers, so that the excellency of the power is of God, and not
of us." Within our earthly weakness, God has deposited His
uncontainable power and demonstrated His unlimited love.

It is in this we find our most excellent treasure through the
Messiah Yeshua: "being pressed on every side, but not com-
pressed; perplexed, but not in despair; persecuted, but not
abandoned; struck down, but not destroyed." Life cuts deep,
and our anguish is profound; yet we are still here, and God is
still saving. As bad as things may be today—as much as we

may hurt and grieve—God continues to restrain our worst destruction.

As we face the agonies of life seemingly alone, let us not overlook the treasure that God stores in us. Indeed, let us "at all times [carry] around in the body the dying of יֵשׁוּעַ, Yeshua, so that the life of יֵשׁוּעַ, Yeshua may also be revealed" in us.

So "do not lose heart. Rather, if our outward man also decays, yet our inward *man* is renewed day by day" (4:16) "For the things seen [today] ARE temporary, but the things not seen ARE age-enduring" (4:18)

Is what God has given you enough? Oh, yes: more than you'll ever need!

PRAYER

I praise You, ADONAI, Allower of tragedy and Permitter of calamity. Though I suffer and strive, Your unmerited favor abounds to me; You hold back my utter destruction. Release the pressure, O God, and untangle my confusion; save me, from the anguish and agony, that my strength may serve You all of my days. Your provision is sufficient, Master. Be glorified in my suffering, and make me worthy to contain Your most infinite and excellent treasure.

LET US CLEANSE OURSELVES

> Having these promises, then, loved ones, let us cleanse ourselves from every pollution of flesh and רוּחַ, ruach, perfecting holiness in the fear of God.
>
> – 2 CORINTHIANS 7:1

The holiness of our God is a revealer. It broadcasts its light, penetrating the shadows of our indecency and exposing every uncleanness. We are embarrassed and ashamed, yet confident in His presence, inviting His holiness to come and wash away our defilement. He draws near, and we breathlessly await His purifying fire...

...and we watch in astonishment as He walks on by.

Wait! Where are You going? Have I not acknowledged my impurity and confessed my need? Why do You turn away, Master? Will You not touch me and make me clean? Please, Holy One! Do not leave me in my filth! I beg You, please! Come back!

ADONAI has mercifully reached down with His outstretched arm of unmerited favor, and, through the sacrifice and rising again of the Son of God, saved us and set us free. We did nothing to deserve it, and can do nothing to improve our righteousness in His sight...

...and so we seek our holiness, expecting it to come in precisely the same way.

Though our sins have been covered, too often we leave our house in disarray, believing it is God's job to clean it up. But we are a temple of ADONAI, who promises to live and walk among us and to be our God. It is therefore *our* responsibility to clean up *ourselves* and rid our temple of all defilement—to "cleanse ourselves from every pollution of flesh and רוּחַ, ruach, perfecting holiness in the fear of God."

Do you desire more than just eternal salvation? Do you want the living, holy presence of God to be active in your life today? Then separate yourself from wickedness and darkness—from unclean things and unequal yokes. Let the holiness of God shine into every shadow of your life, and then cleanse yourself of all that it reveals.

So let us be clean, perfecting our holiness. The responsibility is ours.

PRAYER

ADONAI, awesome in holiness and abundant in unmerited favor, I praise You for Your light of revelation. Shine upon my shadows, God—let the wickedness in my life shriek and shrink in the sight of Your glorious rays of purification. Teach me, Master, to rest in Your salvation, but also to be active in my own cleansing and perfecting. Help me, Yeshua, to rid myself of every pollution, defilement and desecration. Come live and walk in me and be my God, ADONAI, as I make my temple holy for You.

KEPT FROM KNOWING

> But I fear that perhaps as the serpent deceived חַוָּה, Chavah in his cunning, your minds may be corrupted *and kept* from *knowing* the simplicity and the pureness that *IS* in the Messiah. – 2 Corinthians 11:3

There is a certain brand of believers—you know them: satisfied by platitudes, lacking in depth of understanding, seeking God's hand of prosperity without the conviction to be obedient in return. They are shallow in both knowledge and practice; their walk with God appears too simple and superficial, if not non-existent. Indeed, from your point of view, even their salvation seems suspicious...

Not so for you, though, right? You search for the deeper things. Your eyes have been opened to the truth. You have discovered the true goal of the Good News, and successfully restored what was lost to its proper context. Now if only the rest of the Body could see...

Caricatures and over-generalizations aside, some of us tend to consider believers who don't share our views as traitors to the faith. The irony in this, of course, is that we are oblivious to our own compromises and false beliefs, being so convinced of our positions that we are unwilling to question them honestly in light of Scripture. But the only way to pass the speck-in-our-own-eye test is to genuinely evaluate whether our convictions still result in "*knowing* the simplicity and the pureness that is in the Messiah." If your theology requires a lot of creative mental gymnastics, focuses on the backdrop more than the foreground, or—it should go without saying—contradicts Scripture, then "perhaps... your minds may be corrupted," and as much as you trust what you have been told, maybe you have actually been kept from the truth.

There is nowhere that the Deceiver can be more successful than in the minds of believers who are unsatisfied with a simple, straightforward Messiah—who abandon the pure milk of the Good News for the red meat of "deeper study" and hidden things. We must not swing so far from the simple as to forsake objective, essential Scriptural truth, and the beliefs we embrace must be free of the corruption that comes through the cunning theological theories of men.

Don't be deceived by snakes whose teachings obscure "the simplicity and the pureness that *is* in the Messiah." Step back from the serpentine intricacies that lead you away from the plain sense of Scripture, and rediscover the pure and flawless truth of God's simple and perfect word.

PRAYER

Oh, Father, I have seen the hypocrisy and the shallow relationships many have with You. I have looked at my brothers and sisters and judged them for their lack of knowledge and simplistic faith. So I ran toward the "true" teachings that I thought man's religion had kept hidden from me. Have I now kept myself from Your pureness and simplicity? Show me the truth in light of Your word, ADONAI; heal my mind from the corruption caused by false teachings that I currently hold to be true. Help me to be humble and prideless before You, Master, that I may return to and be nourished by Your pure and simple ways…

EXAMINE YOURSELVES

> Test yourselves *to see* if you are in the faith; examine yourselves. Do you yourselves not recognize that יֵשׁוּעַ, Yeshua *the* Messiah is in you, unless, in some respect, you are failing the test? – 2 Corinthians 13:5

You read the Bible and pray. You do not forsake the gathering together of the believers. You praise God with all your heart, and His word is always on your lips...

...and you think that makes you a follower of the Messiah.

For as long as there have been true believers in Yeshua, there have also been imposters and those with a false or incomplete transformation. To be a Messiah-follower—or to look like one—we naturally adopt many outward signs meant to demonstrate an inward belief. But these external evidences can be contrived, or even outright faked—whatever it takes to convince others (and ourselves) that we are indeed true believers. And sometimes, the successful adoption of such outward actions become the entire substance of what we mistakenly think is an actual, strong faith.

This is why we see our spiritual leaders fall into sin, or longtime believers we thought were "on fire" for God appear to suddenly flame out and walk away from the faith. It's not simply because we're human and we are sometimes just overcome by the flesh. It's because we ourselves and those around us allow us to get away with a superficial faith that gives the appearance of depth. It's because sometimes we're really just fake followers... and we had no idea.

"Test yourselves *to see* if you are in the faith; examine yourselves." The goal as a Messiah-follower is not simply to match what you see other believers doing—to adopt certain religious habits or modes of speech, or even to settle in to spiritual routines that, in and of themselves, do have intrinsic value. Instead, test yourself, and do it regularly: How have I been treating others lately? Do I get angry easily? Do I worry too much? What have I been consuming? How do I spend my time, finances and resources? Am I making disciples?

The goal of a true follower of Messiah is not to put on an emotional or mental costume, undergoing an outward lifestyle change that you think will please God and fool your friends. Rather, the goal is for Yeshua the Messiah to be in you—and in you in such a way that you are no longer you at all. "Do you yourselves not recognize that יֵשׁוּעַ, Yeshua *the* Messiah is in you, unless, in some respect, you are failing the test?" Don't be afraid to examine yourself to see if you are really "in the faith." How will you know your condition unless you look?

PRAYER

ADONAI my God, You examine me daily; must I really see for myself? What if I look too closely and find I'm not who I thought I was? Father, I trust Your work in me, whether I fail or pass the test. So upon my self-inspection, Abba, help me to understand and act positively upon the results. Show me, Master, if I am truly "in the faith"... and if I'm not, what I must do to change. You are faithful, Yeshua! Come and live in me, as I seek to live more deeply in You.

THINGS NOT BEING

> [Av'raham is the] father of us all (as it has been written, "I HAVE SET YOU *AS* A FATHER OF MANY ETHNIC-GROUPS") in the sight of Him whom he believed: God, who is bringing the dead to life, and is calling the things not being as being. –ROMANS 4:17

The powerful event of Yeshua's rising again from the dead shattered death, reality and time. It made things formerly impossible now viable; things unheard of now true. It was improbable enough for God to use the tiny nation of Israel—a formerly enslaved and perpetually obstinate people—to bring forth the Messiah of the world. But He also built in to His plan for world-reconciliation a means as confounding to Israel as it is glorious to all the peoples of the earth.

In giving the Torah to Israel, God provided His people with a structure and guide for how to live as a righteous nation before Him. He formed this righteous Israel to serve the Uncircumcised ethnic-groups—the Gentiles—as intermediaries in the reconciliation to their Creator. But the instructions God gave to Israel to teach her His righteous ways turned out to not be what He would actually use to make them righteous. Apparently, it wasn't the doing of God's commands that made or kept Israel right with God, for "God credits righteousness apart from actions" (4:6).

In an astonishing reversal of expectations, the promise turned out to be "not through תּוֹרָה, Torah, but through the righteousness of faith" (4:13). For if our father Av'raham, for example, "was declared righteous by actions, *then* he has *something* to boast *about*" (4:2), rendering any faith empty, and the promises to him useless. "But to him who is not working, yet is believing upon Him who is declaring righteous the ungodly, his faith is credited *to him* to righteousness" (4:5)—not because of any action he does or any command he keeps.

This God of Israel whom we follow—who shatters death, reality and time—is He "who is bringing the dead to life, and is calling the things not being as being." By all appearances, God's promises and righteousness should flow through obedience to the Torah, with no path to God for those who are estranged from those commands. But in reality, God credits righteousness only according to *faith*, making reconciliation with Him available to all who "walk in the steps of the faith of our father אַבְרָהָם, Av'raham" (4:12).

If our God can do all this and more through faith in the Messiah Yeshua, what dead thing in you can He not bring back to life? What thing that is presently *not being* can He not powerfully call forth... and cause it to *be?*

PRAYER

Adonai my God, awesome in power, You confound the wise and make real the impossible. Your ways are far greater and higher than mine, El Shadai; You utterly shatter all of my expectations. There is nothing You cannot do, my Master. You form with Your hand the unlikeliest of nations... You make righteous the unworthiest of vessels—like me. I praise You, O God, for bringing the dead to life; please call Your wondrous things not being as being in me...

BUT GOD PROVES HIS OWN

> For in our still being weak, Messiah—in due time
> —died for the ungodly. For with difficulty will
> anyone die for a righteous man; indeed, for the
> good man, perhaps someone even dares to die. But
> God proves His own love to us: that, in our still
> being sinners, Messiah died for us. –Romans 5:6-8

We know that God loves us... we're almost certain of it. We're sure He's up there somewhere, looking down on us, enveloping us in His love, and watching over our lives. In fact, He's so busy loving everyone that He lets us down from time to time, and our needs go unmet. But that's okay. He still loves us, and we love Him. Love, love, love. Isn't it wonderful? Where are You, God? Don't You love me anymore? I feel so alone...

As life erodes our faith and trust in God, we try to hold on to a vestige of feelings and beliefs in a vain attempt at self-comfort. What we know (or what we believe we know) about God's love often seems at odds with our harsh reality. Yes, ADONAI gives and He takes away—bless the name of ADONAI (Job 1:21). But does He really have to take away so often?

As we struggle to reconcile our thoughts, beliefs and feelings, we inevitably begin to doubt whether God truly loves us at all—or if He ever did. And eventually, we withdraw and fade away from His presence, finding it simpler to disengage and disbelieve than to maintain a belief in the apparently self-contradictory.

Yet through it all—through all the disappointment and discouragement, the successes and victories, the striving and pain —there is only one thought, one belief, that we must retain at all costs:, and it is that "God proves His own love to us: that, in our still being sinners, Messiah died for us." No matter how loved or unloved—how cared for or uncared for—we feel, nothing we experience in this life is as paramount as the next. The proof that He loves us is that He's made us acceptable through Messiah to stand in His unmerited favor.

In Yeshua, we have been "declared righteous in His blood," and we will be "saved through Him from the wrath" that is coming (Romans 5:9). The proof that God loves us is not by always making things go the way we want or expect. It is not by making us happy. No, the proof that He loves us is that while we were His enemies, He reconciled us to Himself through the death of His Son, and then saved us in His life… forever.

PRAYER

O Adonai, how You love me: the lowest of sinners, the greatest of enemies! Remind me, Father, that no matter how near or far I feel from You, Your love for me is beyond measure; Your care for me, unending. Thank You, God, that Your love is unchanging—that it does not wax or wane with either my situation or my feelings. I trust You and believe You, my Master; lead me in the thoughts and the ways of Your abounding and endless love.

WHEN YOU WERE SLAVES

> I speak in the manner of men because of the weakness of your flesh. For even as you presented your members *as* slaves to the uncleanness and to the wickedness—*leading* to the *increasing* wickedness—so now present your members *as* slaves to the righteousness—*leading* to holiness. For when you were slaves of the sin, you were free from the righteousness. –ROMANS 6:19-20

It's hard to be convinced you're in bondage when you walk in unlimited freedom. This is why societies—especially prosperous ones—always eventually cycle back to their deep degradations and perversions. Unfettered, we climb every mountain of corruption and explore every crevasse of deviance—searching for new experiences, conducting unfamiliar experiments of the flesh, excavating uncharted physical and philosophical domains—all while hoping, in vain, for meaning. With such independence and lack of restraint, why would anyone ever conclude they were, in reality, imprisoned by invisible chains? Such is the way of slavery to sin and freedom from all righteousness.

The liberating message of the Good News, then, ironically holds little to no appeal to the sinner. He inherently knows that to follow Yeshua would be to limit his freedom and restrict his movements. He would be unable to act upon every impulse, required instead to curb his thoughts and modify his behavior—an unbearable prison of piousness; a backward internment for a progressive spirit.

But the deceit of evil and the fruit of the flesh are a darkness that blinds the sinner to the constraints of his so-called freedom. In that blackness, he is led about only by base instinct and desire—though he calls it "intellect" and "enlightenment"—and is restrained from the true light that leads to life, being bound by the debt leading to death.

As followers of the Messiah, let us stop willingly resubjugating ourselves to those invisible bonds by failing to fully enslave ourselves to God. Let us relinquish all freedom to do as we please, and instead shut ourselves up to the life-bringing limits of His righteous word. May we be fully convinced of our enslavements, and not be fooled by fleshly freedoms. In the freedom of Messiah, then, let us be truly free... free in the servitude and slavery to our God.

PRAYER

I praise and exalt Your Name, Yeshua, for You have paid the wages of my sin and set me free! Help me, Master, to not seek the darkness again and return to the bonds that deceived me. Cause my fruit to lead to holiness, ADONAI, that my end result will be life age-enduring. Thank You, O God, for fettering the freedom of my flesh, that I may enslave myself freely to You.

THE THINGS OF THE RUACH

> For those who are according to the flesh *set their* mind *on* the things of the flesh, but those *who are* according to the רוּחַ, Ruach *set their mind on* the things of the רוּחַ, Ruach. For the mind of the flesh *is* death, but the mind of the רוּחַ, Ruach *is* life and peace, because the mind of the flesh *is* hostility to God. Indeed, it does not submit... –ROMANS 8:5-7A

We worry, and are anxious; we think about our financial problems, our health, and, sometimes, the inevitabilities of war and death. Meanwhile, thoughts of the latest movie, or what recreational activity we will participate in this weekend, are also occupying our minds. Before long, we take a moment to indulge the spontaneous thoughts generated by our vices, addictions and obsessions. And, of course, we're often simply thinking about ourselves....

It's only natural to have such things swirling around in our heads. Life is physical and corporeal, and we interact with it every moment of our lives. But it's when we engage with life *only naturally* that we reveal our true love. If we are "*set[ting our] mind[s] on* the things of the flesh"—the worries and worldly and carnal things that fill our minds—then we are living not "according to the רוּחַ, Ruach," and are instead serving a master of the material world.

But the mind set on the things of the Ruach thinks none of these things. It's thoughts are submitted to God, not hostile to His guidance and goodness. The mind set on the things of the Ruach does not indulge itself and wander off into pointless and sensual ideas, but rather seeks to please God by resisting worldly and fleshly notions—and the actions that would otherwise follow. The mind set on the things of the Ruach does not lead itself into self-destruction and death, but focuses on light and life and peace. It is fixed upon the rulings and teachings of God—upon the needs and welfare of others, rather than on our own wants and lusts for ourselves.

As servants of our Savior, let us not continue to satisfy either the incessant input and distractions of the world, or the tactile desires of our own flesh, but instead seek the life and peace and right actions in Messiah—and set our minds on the submissive things of the Ruach.

PRAYER

ADONAI, Your ways are ways of life and peace; You fill me with joy in Your presence. Interrupt my mind, Ruach HaQodesh, that I may turn and fix my thoughts on Yours. Forgive me, Father, for entertaining fleshly thoughts and wallowing in my worldly ways. I bow before You, my God, and submit my flesh to Your word of purity and truth, that my mind may be set perfectly and forever on You.

THE IMAGE OF THE INVISIBLE

> *It is He* who rescued us out of the authority of the darkness and transferred *us* into the Reign of the Son of His love (in whom we have the redemption—the forgiveness of the sins), who is the image of the invisible God, first-born of all creation, because in Him were all the things created in the heavens and upon the earth: those visible, and those invisible. –Colossians 1:13-16a

The complete mystery of who God is is beyond all comprehension and intellect. How He can be the Father as distinct from the Son, and yet also be the Son—and further still the Son of Man—is a paradox of truth we must leave for another time. For now, it is sufficient to simply marvel and rest in the glory of His unfathomable mystery—to know that *how* He cares for us is not as immediate for us to understand as the plain and simple fact that He *does*.

For, indeed, what can it be but a glorious mystery that this Son—this man—is "the image of the invisible God"... the same God who created the heavens and the earth and all that is in them? And how can this man have been born into that very creation, yet also have existed "before all," with all things being created and "held together in Him" (1:17)? A man that once was not, yet is God; a God who is not a man, yet dwells fully within Him. He is the first-born over all, yet uncreated; of the creation, yet also the Creator...

...utterly impossible, yet absolutely true.

How this can be true—or even possible—is for mankind to either discount or believe. But for those of us who have such faith, ours is also the equally impossible truth that this God "rescued us out of… darkness and transferred *us* into the Reign of the Son of His love"; that in this Son—in this man—in whom all things were created, "we have the redemption—the forgiveness of the sins."

Truly, it is a mystery beyond all comprehension and intellect that this God should rescue and redeem us in this way. And yet the plain and simple fact is that through this man—who is fully *not* God and yet also fully *is*—He did.

PRAYER

O Yeshua! fully God and fully man—You are the mystery beyond all mysteries! And yet, You do not keep secret from me Your unfathomable and unending redemption, forgiveness and love. I praise You O God, creator of all things, both those visible as well as those invisible. I give You all the glory, ADONAI, for transferring me from the authority of the darkness into Your light. Thank You, Master, for enlightening my heart, that I may believe Your most wondrous, invisible and impossible things…

BEFORE THE FOUNDATION
OF THE WORLD

> Blessed *is* the God and Father of our Master יֵשׁוּעַ,
> Yeshua *the* Messiah, who *has* blessed us with every
> spiritual blessing in the Heavenly places in Mes-
> siah, as He chose us in Him before the foundation
> of the world (for our being holy and unblemished
> before Him). –EPHESIANS 1:3-4

Both resounding confidence and profound humility ought to
be evoked in us at the realization of our being chosen in Messiah "before the foundation of the world." Before we were
born (much less born again); before we were conceived in
the womb; before the existence of every family member we
can trace, and those unknown to our family tree; before the
knitting together of every animal, every blade of grass, every
strand of DNA, every land mass or sea or star in the heavens;
before the very existence of light itself, we were selected... we
were chosen... we were called.

And yet, our being chosen by God was not just some random
act of kindness. He did not select us simply because He knew
what we would one day do or eventually become, and He did
not call us to Himself simply out of His unmerited favor and
boundless love. He chose us for a purpose with an express goal
for our lives: He chose us "for our being holy and unblemished
before Him" as ones acceptable to serve in the courts of the
King.

From before the foundation of the world, God's plan involved
you—the plan "to bring into one *thing* the whole *thing* in the
Messiah" (1:10). Since He has "made known to us the mystery

of His will" (1:9), our job, then, as His holy and unblemished vessels, is to help facilitate "the things in the Heavens and the things upon the earth [being] *brought together* in Him" (1:10). God's goal in us all along was to use us as members of Messiah's Body to reconcile the whole world back to Him.

Are you being holy and blameless in your walk with God and in your normal, everyday life before Him? Set yourself apart from all worldliness today, and allow the blood of Messiah to cover over every blemish. Be confident in your calling and humble in your selection, so that through the Messiah in you, you may fulfill the purpose for which you were conceived in God's mind before the existence and the foundation of all things.

PRAYER

Creator of the universe, how could You have had someone as insignificant as me in mind before You spoke a single thing into existence? Teach me, Father, to not just feel the humility that such a realization deserves, but to know the profound confidence of seeing myself as part of Your unfathomable plan. Thank You, ADONAI, for choosing me—for selecting me as a facilitator of bringing wholeness to Your creation. Now help me, Master, to fully embrace my calling, and to commit myself to Your service... holy and unblemished to You.

THE LOVE OF THE MESSIAH

> For this reason I bow my knees to the Father... so that you may be able in strength to comprehend (with all the קְדוֹשִׁים, Q'doshiym) what *is* the breadth, and length, and height, and depth *of—and* also to know—the love of the Messiah that is exceeding the knowledge, so that you may be filled to all the fullness of God. –EPHESIANS 3:14, 18-19

God loves us—a fact which causes many to respond with affection and affinity toward the Creator. Some perceive it as the love of a father for his child; others still, the endearment of a lover for his love. But to whatever extent God's love is or is not accurately portrayed, what isn't true is the idea that God's love depends on how He feels about us, or we about Him. Love from and for God isn't based on feelings, but on *knowledge.*

To be sure, one would have to be wholly devoid of feelings not to have an emotional response to the incomparable love of God. But we do not become overwhelmed by that love simply because we discern His divinely comforting embrace. Rather, any affirmative response we have ought to come as a result of comprehending—even to the minutest of degrees—"what is the breadth, and length, and height, and depth *of...* the love of the Messiah." When we finally seek to measure the immeasurable ability of God "to do exceedingly abundantly above all things that we ask or think" (3:20), then we will understand love.

God wants us to know the love that exceeds all knowledge, but we can only fathom those unfathomable dimensions when we profess not our feelings, but God's incomprehensible abilities. The Master is longing to "give to you according to the riches of His glory, to be strengthened with power through His Ruach in regard to the inner man, *in order for* the Messiah to dwell through the faith in your hearts" (3:16-17). What God can do—and what He has done—is the display of His infinite love.

Let the Messiah dwell fully in you today, and feel His yearning for and devotion to your soul. But more than that, fully know in the mind of your heart the immeasurable breadth, length, height and depth of His limitless, unknowable love.

PRAYER

O God! I stand before the vastness of Your love, and I am overwhelmed. How can I imagine, Father, much less know, Your unknowable and boundless power, abundance and lovingkindness? I bow my knees in worship, ADONAI, not weighed down by my stresses and troubles, but under the heaviness of Your glory and the lightness of Your load. Cause me to behold Your unlimited ability, my Master, that I may be filled to all the fullness of Your highest, widest and deepest love.

AS CHILDREN OF LIGHT

> [F]or at one time you were Darkness, but now *you are* Light in the Master. As children of Light, walk (for the fruit of the Light *is* in all goodness and righteousness and truth, proving what is well-pleasing to the Master), and have no partnership with the unfruitful actions of the Darkness, but rather even refute *them*. –EPHESIANS 5:8-11

Why would you choose to walk in the dark when you are able to walk in the light? Maybe it is early in the morning, before dawn, and you don't wish to awaken a slumbering loved one. Or perhaps you are out of doors, away from the city, off in the desert or the mountains, where light is a hindrance to watching the beautiful, clear night sky.

But what if it is daytime, the sun is out, and all are awake? For what reason would you shut out the light and welcome the dark? Or, what if it is night, when light would be a helpful assistant? Why would you instead seek a poorly lit room, a back alley, or the cover of darkness?

Whether a particular darkness is good or evil, light is always its disrupter. And when light threatens to shine upon an un-righteousness done in secret, that secret will always desire to seek out a deeper darkness.

Yet as followers of the Messiah Yeshua, we are now "children of Light... and have no partnership with the unfruitful actions of the Darkness." When we seek out darkness during the times when light would be more fitting, it should serve as a sign that we are desiring to conceal something our souls want kept secret. Darkness should be a time for rest, not action—a time to hold back our foot, not to walk. So if it is in the absence of light that we are active, then it is worth questioning why, and whether it is bringing us to good or to shame.

"As children of Light," then, "walk," so that you may not stumble into the evil awaiting you in the darkness. And should you find yourself lurking about in the shadows, take care to remember: you're only keeping secrets from yourself.

PRAYER

Adonai my God, Father of Light, shine upon me and pierce the darkness of my life. Show me how I have been partnering with secret, unfruitful actions, rather than bearing the fruit of the Light that is only in goodness, righteousness and truth. Help me, Master, to refute and rebuke the unspeakable actions in me that seek out the cover of darkness. Draw me, Yeshua, to the revelation of Your pure and beautiful radiance, so that I may be well-pleasing in Your Light alone... and for all of my days, may walk.

THAT I MAY GAIN MESSIAH

> But what things were gains to me, these I have counted *to be* loss because of the Messiah. Yes, indeed, and I count all things to be loss because of the excellency of *having* a knowledge of Messiah יֵשׁוּעַ, Yeshua my Master—because of whom I suffered the loss of all things, and consider them to be excrement—so that I may gain Messiah...
>
> –PHILIPPIANS 3:7-8

Giving your life to Yeshua is an attractive proposition when you consider all there is to gain from it. By following Him, we receive the gift and promise of eternal life, which, by itself, ought to be more than enough. But in practice, many of us tend toward a conditional allegiance. We are more likely to love God and pay attention to what He says when He's also prospering us in *this* life, and the price for our obedience is the God-funded compensation of greater abundance, comfort and happiness.

While such things are clearly granted by and attributable to God, and we should be thankful and grateful whenever He prospers us, there is no divine law that says self-serving obedience to God causes prosperity—especially not our *individual* blessing. On the contrary, as Messiah-followers, our attitudes toward success in health, wealth and happiness should not be based on what we have to *gain*, but rather, "what things were gains to [us], these [we should] count... *to be* loss because of the Messiah."

And why should this be so? Because everything in this life is *nothing* compared to "the excellency of *having* a knowledge of

Messiah יֵשׁוּעַ, Yeshua [our] Master." Indeed, we are to "count all things to be loss"—to "consider them to be excrement"—because knowing Yeshua is the most excellent thing that God offers us in both this life and the next. Living for Messiah, regardless of either blessing or suffering, is what matters. Knowing Yeshua—not material or emotional abundance—is the greatest gain.

Our reward as followers of Messiah is not valued according to the prosperity, blessing and favor we receive, but by what we are willing to give up to fully follow the Messiah. Accept all blessings and abundance with gratitude and thanksgiving, but do not covet them as compensation for your obedience. The prize goes not to those who seek the greatest gain, but to those whose heart's desire is to be the biggest loser.

PRAYER

Oh Father, I do feel like a loser... for seeing abundance as evidence of Your love, and loss as proof of Your displeasure. But You are not a fickle manipulator, ADONAI, dangling prosperity before me as incentive for my obedience! All that I have gained, my Master, I now throw down and count as loss, so that I may gain and be found in You. I praise You, Yeshua: the greatest reward of all. Help me to truly become the biggest loser for You...

THAT THEY MAY BE
SOUND IN THE FAITH

> This testimony is true, for which reason *you must* refute them sharply, so that they may be sound in the faith, not paying attention to Jewish myths and commands of men, turning themselves away from the truth. –TITUS 1:13-14

These days, unless we're a busybody or a legalist, most of us keep to ourselves. We stay within our own bubbles, not getting seriously involved in others' existences, if we happen to notice their being there at all. So we walk with God largely alone, not delving too deep even with our fellow believers. And when we catch one of them in a mindset or behavior that is contrary to the word, we bite our tongues and stick our heads in the sand, hoping no one will notice that we know.

But in a fully functioning Body, this wouldn't be the case at all. We would address bad behavior and empty, deceptive talk—not for the purpose of inserting ourselves into people's lives, but in order to get them to *stop*. Lest we think it's not our place to interfere, as fellow-followers of the Master Yeshua, it is not only our right, but our duty. We cannot permit falseness and sin to go unanswered anymore than we can allow a physical infection to go uneradicated.

So when we see our fellow-believers (or family or friends) begin "turning themselves away from the truth," inaction is not actually an available option, and prayer is not enough. Yet while we have a clear responsibility to confront and challenge such unrighteousness, it is not so that *we* can meddle in others' affairs, but so that *they* "may be sound in the faith." That is why, when kind correction is not received, we are commanded to "refute them sharply." The strong admonition is for *their* sake—to turn them back for their own good.

If you truly walk in the Messiah's love, you will not stand idly by as your fellow-believers go astray. Love does not demand ignorance or tolerance, but confrontation and, if necessary, sharp rebuke. It is better to be hated for speaking the truth than loved for keeping quiet. As long as you are acting in unselfish love, don't worry about butting in to others' affairs. Be nosy if you must—be forceful if you have to—but involve yourself voluntarily for the sake of their souls.

PRAYER

Abba, as I live my quiet life and tend to my own things, help me also to not look the other way when I see Your children turning from the truth. Press me down in lowliness, Father, yet raise me up in boldness to always speak Your word in love. Make me fearless, ADONAI, that I may not avoid confrontation and conflict; make me humble, that I will not seek it out for my own manipulative purposes. Whether in gentle correction or sharp rebuke, fill me with purity of heart and the desire only to help return all Your lost ones to You.

TO RESCUE GODLY ONES

> ...ADONAI has known *how* to rescue godly ones out of *ways of* testing, and to watch over unrighteous ones to a Day of Judgment... –בּ כֵּיפָא 2 KEIFA 2:9

God's righteous judgment will not be denied. He does not let the sinner go unpunished—even fallen Messengers ("angels") He will not spare (2:4). ADONAI's justice will always, in the end, be satisfied; His judgment will always prevail. He will make an example of the ungodly, but the godly He will guard and deliver.

Consider Noach who escaped the destruction of the entire ancient world. He alone was righteous in that generation, resisting its corruption, and obeying all of God's commands. ADONAI immersed that world and washed away its sin... but Noach, the godly one, He rescued.

Consider Lot who escaped the judgment of S'dom and 'Amorah: had there been ten men like him, those cities would have been spared. Though Lot's soul was being tormented, "seeing and hearing *the conduct*, living among them day by day with *their* wrongful actions" (2:8), he remained righteous, his serious flaws notwithstanding. ADONAI reduced those cities to ashes... but Lot, the godly one, He rescued.

Like righteous Noach and Lot, we too, as followers of the Messiah Yeshua, must daily take God's test. In this world, we are faced with the moment by moment decision of whether to allow ourselves to be drawn in to its sinful, sensual, fleshly, unrighteous, unprincipled and ungodly ways, or whether to righteously resist their pull. No amount of reason or will power can keep us from the degradation and destruction that awaits all who give in. Only our trust in and reliance upon the Holy One will save us from the coming, engulfing flames.

Do not grow weary of taking the test. God is proving you for your own sake, so that you will know whether you are trusting Him or not. No matter the temptation, no matter the trial, count on God and wait expectingly for His rescue. Don't give in to the lures of the moment, but be ready for the exam of your life.

PRAYER

ADONAI, righteous and Holy One, Your perfect judgment will not be denied. Surely, You forever punish the wicked, O God, but Your godly ones You will never fail. Your ways of testing are hard, Master, but please show me both my weaknesses and Your strength. Rescue me from this world, Yeshua; make me holy and godly before You. Help me, Abba, that I may remain in You every moment, and easily pass every test.

AND THE WORD WAS GOD

> In the beginning was the Word, and the Word was
> with God, and the Word was God; this One was
> in the beginning with God. –יוֹחָנָן YOCHANAN I:I-2

"In the beginning of God's creating the heavens and the earth,
the earth had been nothingness and emptiness, and darkness
WAS on the face of the deep, and the רוּחַ אֱלֹהִים, Ruach 'Elohiym
was fluttering on the face of the waters…

"…and God said…" (בְּרֵאשִׁית B'RESHIYT I:I-3)

In the beginning, all the things that happened happened
through the Word. "Not even one thing happened that has
happened" (יוֹחָנָן Yochanan 1:3) which the Word did not utter
into existence. In a universe of nothingness, the Word spoke,
"and light was" (בְּרֵאשִׁית B'reshiyt 1:3). In a world of emptiness, the Word spoke, and the heavens came to be. The Word
spoke, and all the waters of the earth were collected together
in one place; the Word spoke, and the world exploded and
teemed with life.

This Word was not simply *there* "in the beginning." The Word
did not merely speak God's mind and inform the animation
of that untouched creation. This Word—*the* Word—was not
just some pronouncement of the Creator, proceeding from
His mouth in mindless, lifeless obedience. Indeed, Life itself
was in the Word, because the Word was much more than
"with God"—the Word Himself "was God."

"And the Word became flesh and dwelt among us" (יוֹחָנָן Yochanan 1:14) in the very world that "was made through Him"
(1:10). The One who was with God, and who was God, emp-

tied Himself to become like us—the Creating One joining with the created. No God has greater power and compassion than the One who would deny Himself of Himself for our acceptance. He gives Life, He gives Light, He is the glorious Word of Creation; He is One, He is God, He is... Yeshua.

PRAYER

Glorious and Holy Creating One—one and only of a father— You alone are full of unmerited favor and truth! I receive Your Life and Your Light, my Master—powerfully speak them into existence in me. O Word of God become flesh, shine deeply into my darkness that I may perceive Your brilliant and surrounding light of salvation. Reconcile me to Yourself— recreate me in Your image. Yeshua, let Your word be creative in me.

LOOK! THE LAMB

> These things came to pass in בֵּית־עַנְיָה, Beit-An'yah, beyond the יַרְדֵּן, Yar'den, where יוֹחָנָן, Yochanan was immersing. On the next day, he saw יֵשׁוּעַ, Yeshua coming to him, and said, "Look! the Lamb of God, who is taking away the sin of the world!"
>
> –יוֹחָנָן YOCHANAN 1:28-29

They all knew how it would end. Though perhaps they didn't want to believe it, and could barely conceive it, and scattered in fear and remorse when it happened, Yeshua's destiny was made clear from the beginning: His death was the door through which the world would be saved.

Before the Master had done a single thing to announce that the Messiah—the Son of God—had come, Yochanan the Immerser publicly declared Yeshua to be "the Lamb of God, who is taking away the sin of the world." The imagery is unmistakable; the inference, unavoidable. Only a lamb that has been slaughtered—a lamb whose life is taken—can fulfill the purpose of having its life transferred to ours... whether for consumption or for sacrifice. But like the covering blood of the Passover lambs, whose blood stained the doorways of God's enslaved people in Egypt, this Lamb's blood would be shed for our sins, and, as from slavery, cause us to be set free.

This man who is a "lamb"—who is "in front" because He was "before" (1:15)—walked and taught and served and lived, all so that He could give His life for yours. Though we should not be surprised at this singular act of love, His sacrifice is nevertheless astonishing, and no amount of foreknowledge is enough to outweigh the reality of His shocking and death-defying feat.

The Lamb of God has come to take away your sin, but He will not wrestle it from your stubborn grasp. As the Messiah surrendered Himself to death at the hands of men, surrender all your sin to Him today, and find resurrection life in the hands of God. We all know how this is ultimately going to end. It's time to choose the door that leads to life so that yours may be consumed by His.

PRAYER

Lamb of God, so humble and lowly in heart, You take away my sin in loving-kindness and unmerited favor. Your sacrifice is no surprise to me, Master, for You died the same way You lived—in selflessness and breathtaking power. Consume me, O Holy One, and leave none of me left; I willingly hand myself over for Your refining. Cleanse me, Yeshua, thoroughly washing my head, hands and feet. Take me into Your death that I may be raised up to life in You forever.

THAT I MAY DO HIS WILL

> Meanwhile, His disciples were asking Him, saying, "רַבִּי, Rabiy, eat." But He said to them, "I have food to eat that you have not known." The disciples then said one to another, "Did anyone bring Him anything to eat?" יֵשׁוּעַ, Yeshua said to them, "My food is that I may do the will of Him who sent Me, and may finish His work. Do not say that it is four more months, and *then* the harvest comes. Look! I say to you: lift up your eyes and see the fields, that they are white toward harvest already."
>
> –יוֹחָנָן Yochanan 4:31-34

A father, desperate for his son's healing, went away to seek out Yeshua. When he found Him, he implored the Master to return home with him before his deathly ill child died. Neither refusing nor complying, Yeshua simply disconfirmed the man's reality. "Be going on—your son lives," the Master said, and "the man believed the word that יֵשׁוּעַ, Yeshua said to him" (4:50).

And on the way he was met with the news that his son, indeed, was alive.

The Master said that "My food is that I may do the will of Him who sent Me, and may finish His work." Elaborating further, He exhorted His disciples to not say that it is "four more months, and *then* the harvest comes," but rather to "see the fields, that they are white toward harvest already."

Like the father who believed that his son was alive simply by a word from Yeshua, the Master is teaching us to see what is not yet there as there, and to not procrastinate in acting upon that expectation. He wants us to believe it before we see it. He wants us to take action now, counting on God to provide for and meet us exactly where and when we need Him, according to His will.

Unless our only hunger is to do the will and the work of the Father, will we neither sow nor reap in faith. We need to be so desperate for His sustenance that we will act solely upon our trust in things that are not yet there. Starve yourself today of hopes and dreams that are based on wishful thinking or the reasoning and intellect of man. Instead, welcome the hunger pangs for God—allow them to drive you to get up and move—and then act in faith, expecting His nourishment to arrive at exactly the perfect time.

PRAYER

Father, I lift up my eyes to see the fields around me, yet, I confess: I see only fallow ground. Help me, God, to perceive them already white toward harvest, as You assure my soul that it will be. Master Yeshua, as You have feasted on the will and work of the Father, grow in me the same insatiable hunger to do only Your work according to Your will. ADONAI, fill me with perfect desperation for You, that I may always see and act upon what is not yet, believing it is there already.

THE BREAD OF YOUR LIFE

> יֵשׁוּעַ, Yeshua said to them, "I am the bread of the
> Life; he who is coming to me will not hunger, and
> he who is believing in me will not thirst—at any
> time." –יוֹחָנָן YOCHANAN 6:35

The now and not yet of believing in Yeshua can often be a
difficult walk to navigate. On the one hand, we have the
solemn promise and expectation of life age-enduring, when
all is restored, healed and perfect. On the other hand, we
have to continue to contend with life today, along with all the
challenges, hardships, hills and valleys it brings. We experience the realities of day-to-day life while holding on to the
promises of forever, and from time to time we see eternity
seep backward to enlighten our everyday existence.

So when the Master Yeshua tells us that whoever comes to
Him will not hunger, and whoever believes in Him will not
thirst, it has the potential to elicit two distinct and divergent
responses within us. One is to completely believe it to the
rejection of our actual physical reality and circumstances.
The other is to sincerely doubt it, as evidenced by that same
physical reality. How can we admit we are hungry if God has
promised we will no longer hunger? How can we deny our
thirst when we are, indeed, still thirsty?

But this is the false dichotomy: that no one can reach for
eternity while at the same time dancing with his present
circumstances. The two are hopelessly and mutually exclusive,
we think, and if one of them exists, then the other simply
cannot be. Yet this is exactly the kind of faith we must hold
onto and act upon: the kind that denies the false dichotomy;

the kind that simultaneously accepts and disbelieves our physical reality.

There is no lie or contradiction or false hope in the Master's promise. There is no assurance for the future at the expense of the present. Though it may often be a struggle to tangibly see, it is the truth that we must nevertheless enact and believe. In Messiah, neither the present nor the future are our only, lonely realities. In Yeshua—"at any time"—the not yet is also now, and it is up to us whether to accept and navigate that new reality... both forever and today.

PRAYER

Father, to my natural mind, this is nothing but nonsense. Yet I know that Your promises are not only for eternity, but also for my life in You today. Help me, Master, to walk equally in the now and not yet—to neither deny nor accept any reality in opposition to Your word. Teach me, God, how to touch the intangible—to reach the unreachable—through a faith that transcends my perceptions. I praise You, Yeshua, the bread of my Life—for only in You will I neither hunger nor thirst again.

NOT OF THIS WORLD

> Then the יְהוּדִים, Y'hudiym said, "Will he kill himself? For he said, 'Where I go away, you are not able to come.'" And He said to them, "You are from below; I am from above. You are of this world; I am not of this world. Therefore, I said to you that you will die in your sins—for if you do not believe that I am *HE*, you will die in your sins." –יוֹחָנָן YOCHANAN 8:22-24

There He is, right in front of me—so close, I could reach out and touch Him. But instead, I will stand here and resist. I will argue, and talk back, and challenge everything He says. What authority does this One have, anyway? How dare He testify of Himself? Who does this guy think He is?

Now He is issuing this strange warning to me. What do I care if He goes away? Why would I want to follow where He goes? No matter what He thinks, you can believe I certainly won't be looking for Him. Maybe He'll just go ahead and kill Himself. One can only hope.

Wait—*I'm* the one who's going to die? When did we start talking about life and death, here? Hold on a minute. Say all those things you were saying again. Hey, where are you going? Please! Stop! I don't want to die! Wait! Come back!

When man argues with God, he can be assured he is missing the point. We can try changing the subject, poking holes in His argument, even shooting the messenger. None of it changes the fact that by dismissing whatever He says, we are only dooming ourselves.

Yeshua Himself is God's message—a Word that is "not of this world." As long as man holds arrogantly to his own position, unwilling to consider the inconceivable, he will one day find himself out of time. God is God, men are men, and all mankind has sinned. But we no longer have to die in our sins. It's not too late to believe Yeshua is the only One who can save us. Let us swallow our pride, lift up our eyes, and start looking for Him like our life depended on it. And from where He is, He will surely find us… and to there we will be able to go.

PRAYER

O Yeshua, Messiah of Israel, I do believe that You are He. Save me, ADONAI, from dying in my sin, that I may live with You forever. Humble me, my Savior, that I may seek You always; thank You, Light of the World, that I am not too late. Accept my service, Master, for as long as I live, that I may worship and follow wherever You go.

NOW I SEE

> So for a second time they called the man who was
> blind, and they said to him, "Give glory to God.
> We have known that this man is a sinner." Then
> he answered, "If he is a sinner, I have not known.
> One thing I have known: that being blind, now I
> see." –יוֹחָנָן YOCHANAN 9:24-25

A little clay, a little water, and the Master had opened those long-closed eyes. He was a man born blind, but now he could see... all kinds of things.

The P'rushiym were incredulous. How could this healer be from God, since he did this powerful act on the Shabbat? Yet how is a "sinful one... able to do such signs?" (9:16). They interrogated the man—twice. They questioned his parents ("[He] was born blind? How then does he now see?") (9:19). They breathed threats of putting anyone out of the synagogue who professed this healer to be Messiah. They pressured the man to renounce his miraculous physician.

"What did he do to you? How did he open your eyes?" (9:26), they grilled him repeatedly. The man answered, "I told you already, and you did not hear. Why do you want to hear *it* again?" (9:27). And in that moment the man born blind saw more than he had ever seen before. He saw their rage, their fear, their dread—their need—and he replied, to their complete horror, "Do you also want to become his disciples?" (9:27).

The P'rushiym became irate, exploding in defensiveness, as the man asserted again and again the one indisputable fact before them—that once "being blind, now [he could] see." This was a truth for which his opponents clearly had no vision.

When Yeshua tries to open our eyes to His reality, it is only our own willfulness, stubbornness, arrogance and fear that keep us in the dark. Like the P'rushiym seeking insight from a man born blind, no answer within ourselves can shed light on God's truth. Only when we submit our will to that of the Master can we recognize our transparent attempts to remain in control of our lives. We must, instead, relinquish all allegiance to ourselves and, once and for all, "want to become his disciples" (9:27).

PRAYER

Master Yeshua, healer of men born blind, truly You are of God. Open my eyes and cause me to see You, that I may believe and trust You with my whole life. Help me, Father, to submit my will to Your ways—to not continue to lead myself about as if I could actually see. I worship You, ADONAI, and give You all the glory, for without You I am completely blind. Please teach me now how to see.

I AM THE RISING AGAIN

> Then מַרְתָּא, Mar'ta said to יֵשׁוּעַ, Yeshua, "Master, if You had been here, my brother would not have died. But even now, I have known that whatever You ask of God, God will give to You." יֵשׁוּעַ, Yeshua said to her, "Your brother will rise again." מַרְתָּא, Mar'ta said to Him, "I have known that he will rise again, in the Rising Again in the Last Day." יֵשׁוּעַ, Yeshua said to her, "I am the Rising Again, and the Life. He who is believing in Me, even if he dies, will live." –יוֹחָנָן YOCHANAN 11:21-25

Yeshua's beloved friend El'azar had already been four days dead. When He had first received the news, He spoke to His disciples as if El'azar was merely asleep, and He showed no urgency to get to him. When He finally arrived, El'azar's sister Mar'ta went out to meet Him, grieved that Yeshua had not been there to keep El'azar alive. Yeshua comforted her, saying that El'azar would rise again, and Mar'ta tried her best to believe.

Mar'ta's hope and expectation for El'azar was somewhat convoluted. She seemed to express a deep belief in Yeshua, but, nevertheless, didn't make all the connections. She claimed to know and believe that God would grant Yeshua whatever He asked, implying that if Yeshua wanted to bring El'azar back to life, He could. Yet when Yeshua spoke of El'azar rising again, Mar'ta merely responded by professing her belief of the Last Days. And when Yeshua asked her if she believed that "He who is believing in Me, even if he dies, will live," Mar'ta replied, "Yes, Master, I have believed that You are the Messiah, the Son of God, who is coming to the world" (11:27).

Ultimately, she would question the Master when He asked for El'azar's tomb to be opened. So what, exactly, did Mar'ta actually believe and understand?

When we come to Yeshua with our needs, we know full well what God can do. Yet, sometimes we are afraid to hope, and defer instead to the beliefs that cannot let us down. Yes, there will be a rising again in the Last Days, and, yes, Yeshua is the Messiah, the Son of God. These truths bring us comfort and hope for the future—as well they should. But, perhaps like Mar'ta, we sometimes use them to let us off the hook for *today*, allowing us to lower our expectations of God, so that we are not disappointed when He seems to be taking His time… or not there at all.

Today is the day to believe that Yeshua is the Messiah and the Son of God, that He is the Rising Again and the Life, and that whoever is believing in Him—even if he dies today— may return to *this* life tomorrow. Don't be afraid to ask God for what you need; know that He can give it… by His will, in His time.

PRAYER

O Yeshua, "even now, I have known that whatever You ask of God, God will give to You." Teach me to not lower my expectations, Master, allowing myself to only trust You for future tomorrows. You are "the Rising Again, and the Life," and "I have believed that You are the Messiah, the Son of God, who is coming to the world" (11:27). Help me, Yeshua, to not be afraid to believe You now for the miraculous things You are willing to do in me today.

YOU CAME TO THIS MOMENT

> "Now My soul has been troubled, and what? will
> I say, 'Father, save me from this moment'? Rather,
> because of this, I came to this moment. Father,
> glorify Your Name." –יוֹחָנָן YOCHANAN 12:27-28A

The Master Yeshua "was not sent except to the lost sheep of
the house of יִשְׂרָאֵל, Yis'rael" (Matit'yahu 15:24), so it was apparently momentous when certain Greeks, who had come to
Y'rushalayim for the Pesach, were asking to see Him. To this
the Master responded, saying, "The time has come that the
Son of Man may be glorified" (12:23). The occurrence of this
particular event, at this particular time, triggered Yeshua's
realization that the moment He had been dreading was at
hand. God's endgame was now in motion.

Though He would later agonize more deeply over the sacrifice
He would soon endure, for now, Yeshua would only stop long
enough to recognize and admit that His soul was "troubled,"
and to ponder what He might do about it. The first thing that
crossed His mind was to ask the Father to save Him. Though
such a request is always a viable option, it was a notion He
quickly dismissed. Rather, instead of seeking a way out, the
Master committed to moving closer to His disconcerting
destiny. He knew that "because of this," He had come to this
very moment.

But what if Yeshua *had* asked the Father to save Him... and the
Father did it? What if Yeshua *had* instead turned away from
His sacrifice... and it never happened? It would have left us
dead in our sins, without God, and waiting for a salvation that
would never come. Yet when the moment came for Yeshua to

choose whether to sidestep His gruesome, glorifying destiny or to steadfastly go through with it, the Master understood that everything that had happened had been leading to this moment. He knew that, because of His destiny, the moment to choose had now come.

There are times when we need to call out to the Father and ask Him to save us—to step in and alter the course of our lives. And there are times to acknowledge that He has brought us to this place and time—even to that which is dreadful—that we may eventually fulfill His purpose for us. We must not be squeamish or afraid to face those times, but rather realize that the Father brings us to every moment. How we respond to those moments is a test of our character, revealing whether we will trust the Father or not.

Don't be afraid to walk through soul-troubling times. He has brought you here for this very hour... now glorify His Name.

PRAYER

ADONAI, I praise You for Your salvation—for Your ready hand of deliverance and Your steadfast will to save. I thank You, Father, for choosing me to serve You and to fulfill a purpose that will glorify Your Name. Teach me, Master, to have confidence You are there, but to not run to You for escape when You have called me to persevere. Thank You, God, for not leaving me on my own. You bring me to every moment, and You never fail to bring me through.

DO YOU KNOW THE WAY?

> "And if I go on and prepare a place for you, I will come again and will receive you to Myself, so that where I am, you may be also. And where I am going, you have known the way." תּוֹמָא, Toma said to Him, "Master, we have not known where You are going; how are we able to know the way?" יֵשׁוּעַ, Yeshua said to him, "I am the way, and the truth, and the life; no one comes to the Father unless through Me." –יוֹחָנָן YOCHANAN 14:3-6

One day it will all be over—for you, for everyone else, and for the entire physical world. When it is done, some of us will have a new place to go; the rest of us will not be invited. For those who are going, the Master Yeshua has already gone there to prepare that place and make it ready. But in order to get there, first, we need to know the way.

Some of us hope to find the way by being good—by doing good deeds for others, and being tolerant of those who are different. Others of us will look for the way through religion—by routine attendance of worship services and devotion to the forms and traditions therein. Others still will expect to find the way buried within the Scriptures—hidden deep beneath the plain and simple—awaiting its discovery by the true student of God's word. Yet no actions, efforts or motives—invaluable, neutral or otherwise—will provide us with a direct path upon which to make our way to that final place.

It is a place both unfindable and unfathomable, yet easily discovered; beyond both our reach and comprehension, yet within our grasp. We cannot get there through our sheer will; we will never arrive there without our complete compliance. How, then, can we follow Him there? How, now, are we able to know the way?

If our heart's desire is to live forever with Yeshua in the place He has prepared for us, then the only way to get there is by knowing the Way—the Master—Himself. We must immerse ourselves in His teachings, share in His sufferings, and take up His execution stake to bear as our own. When we truly know the Master's character, purpose, priorities and goals, it changes who we are—how we think and behave—laying out before us the perfect path of our life. It is a narrow road with no room for our own preferences and propensities. We must lay them down and then put on the Messiah, following faithfully in His footsteps.

Only through Yeshua may we come to the place He has gone away to prepare for us. The truth and the life lie along the way of the Master...

...are you willing—and ready—to follow?

PRAYER

Adonai, Your ways are not my ways, and I need Your help to find You. Take me to live forever in Your house, Father; make me worthy of permanent residence. Show me how my efforts to reach You fall short from a lack of knowing You, Yeshua. Open my eyes, Master, that I may truly know You and walk the narrow way, and that I may find the only truth—and my only life—eternally in You.

YOU ARE THE BRANCHES

> "I am the vine; you *are* the branches. He who is remaining in Me, and I in him—this one bears much fruit, because apart from Me you are not able to do anything." –יוֹחָנָן YOCHANAN 15:5

As the Body of Messiah grows increasingly individualistic, each member focusing mostly on his own relationship with God, one has to wonder whether we are slowly dying on the vine, or if we were cut off a long time ago. Seeking God personally and looking to improve our lives is healthy and good, but not if it's done for self-serving reasons. Following Yeshua means serving God, serving God means bearing fruit, and bearing fruit means serving others—contributing to the life and health of the whole vine.

When we see our life in Messiah merely in terms of what we expect God to do for us in exchange for our devotion, we have reduced His purposes for us to a fruitless, self-centered orbit. What no one told you was that God cannot abide such a fruitless branch—on the contrary, it sucks the life out of the entire vine. Indeed, when there is a branch in Messiah that is not bearing fruit—one that is more concerned for itself than the other members of the Body; one that is not contributing to others' lives and health above its own—the Father "takes it away." He cuts off and casts aside that dead branch, so that the remaining plant will flourish in its place.

Being fruitful for Messiah, however, is not an easy proposition, as fruitfulness is also accompanied by pain. While the fruitless branch is completely and ruthlessly removed, the fruitful branch does not escape the farmer's shears, but is carefully pruned. Strategically cutting back twisted and crowded growth, the Father makes the fruitful branch clean, preparing it to blossom and thrive in future seasons and making it ready to be an increasingly productive part of the whole. To be fruitless and cut off, or to be fruitful and pruned back—either way, we face the shears... but only one way do we continue to grow.

The Master teaches us that we will "bear... much fruit," but only if we remain in Him—the vine. As branches of the one united vine, we benefit from and contribute to the entire organism—the whole Body of Messiah. We need to recognize that our connection to Yeshua extends to and depends upon everyone else who is connected to Him, and not allow an exclusive focus on ourselves to cut us off from Yeshua.

He is the vine, and we *collectively* form His branches. How will you fare against the Father's shears?

PRAYER

Master Yeshua, I have sought with my whole heart to remain in You... but where did all these other branches come from? All this time, I have focused on myself—on my personal relationship with You—not realizing what a drain I might actually be on Your whole Body. Do not take me away, Father, but instead prune me—cause me temporary injury—that I may grow to become a selfless, fruitful branch in Your flourishing vine. Teach me, Master, to no longer see myself as an individual limb, but to put the interests of the whole vine ahead of my own, and to bear abundant fruit for You.

THAT THEY ALL MAY BE ONE

> "And I do not ask in regard to these alone, but also in regard to those believing in me through their word, that they all may be one, as You, Father, *ARE* in me, and I in You—that they also may be in us, so that the world may believe that You sent me."
>
> –יוֹחָנָן YOCHANAN 17:20-21

There may be as many as 45,000 Christian denominations worldwide. Let that sink in for a moment. Forty-five *thousand*. Mind you, these are not just different cultural expressions of every nation, language and tribe, but thousands upon thousands of autonomous and distinct faith traditions—including different ways of interpreting and applying the Scriptures. This says nothing, of course, of the innumerable nuances in belief that many denominations accept among their members—a reality reflected nowhere more than in the various streams of "Hebrew Roots" teachings and within the Messianic Jewish movement. Affiliated or independent, true believers or otherwise, today's Body of Messiah is, sadly, nothing if not *divided*.

The problem, however, is not religion itself, but the people who practice it. Step one: do not hold to the Scriptures as the sole, binding standard. Step two: reinterpret various passages of Scripture based on your own reasoning or a new "revelation." Step three: break fellowship over it and go start something else. This obviously wild oversimplification is basically how denominations (and, often, congregations) are made. People think they're smarter or more spiritual or more correct than one another—and, apparently, more than the Author as well—and after failing to change minds, they just change venues. It is a flawless process to endlessly fracture the unity of Messiah's Body.

A certain amount of physical disconnection is obviously to be expected. We are naturally separated by geography, and any given home or house of worship can only hold so many people at a time. But these are not the barriers that contribute most acutely to division within the Body. Rather, we err by not focusing on what unites us, while simultaneously tolerating conflicting opinions and ideas. We are so accustomed to disunity that we no longer put in the work to become of one mind on matters to which the Scriptures speak. We do not allow the Scriptures alone to mediate our disputes, but rather prefer to keep our own counsel.

The Master's prayer for us—we who would believe in Him through the word of His emissaries—was that we would be set apart from the world, and gathered together with one another in life, in holiness and in unity. The Scriptures have no prescription for division; God's word has no vision for denominations. Those inventions are our own. Rather, through the word, we are supposed to be united "so that the world may believe"—we are supposed to walk together in the truth of Yeshua—undivided... as one.

PRAYER

Father, set Your people apart in the truth; Your word is truth. Let us no longer be separated by pride and wrong-headed thinking that antagonizes the sole and flawless standard of Your word. Help us, Master, to "all say the same thing," that we may be "perfectly united in the same mind and in the same judgment" (1 Corinthians 1:10). Cause us to humbly submit to Your will and to Your word. Make us one, ADONAI, and let it begin with me.

THEY DID NOT YET UNDERSTAND

> Then, therefore, the other disciple who came first
> to the tomb also entered, and he saw and believed,
> for they did not yet understand the Scripture, that
> it was necessary for Him to rise again out of the
> dead. –יוֹחָנָן YOCHANAN 20:8-9

The Scriptures had been fulfilled: Yeshua had risen again out
of the dead... yet the disciples still did not understand. When
word came from Mir'yam that the Master had been taken
away out of the tomb, Keifa and "the other disciple" quickly
ran there only to find it empty—save Yeshua's linen clothes
and head cloth. They had now seen with their eyes and believed in their minds that the Master, indeed, was gone. So
why was it so hard to understand that Yeshua was alive?

It didn't help, of course, that the disciples were often relatively
dense, and the Master Himself had the tendency to speak
somewhat indirectly at times. But usually, He would eventually spell out particularly important points that He wanted
them to grasp—much like the Scriptures He embodies. As
long as the disciples were able count to three (as in, "three
days"), one would think they could have figured out what was
going on. But when the time came, they were seriously perplexed, despite both the evidence before them, and, perhaps
more importantly, the divine notification they had received
beforehand.

Much like those closest to the Master, we often insist on seeing
and understanding things *before* we will commit to a belief.
"If I'm supposed to believe that Yeshua rose again, that He
is the Messiah and the Son of God, that He wants me to die

to myself daily, take up His execution stake, and abide by the Scriptures without compromise—letting them completely rule my life—*well, then, prove it.* Show me, so that I can see it with my own eyes; bring me the evidence so that I can understand." And yet, even when everything adds up and we are presented with the proof, seeing doesn't always bring understanding... so we continue to refuse to believe.

As long as we place understanding before belief, we will never truly walk in faith... and that's the way He likes it. Though the word of God is often puzzling and roundabout, it does not fail to speak directly to us where it matters most, revealing beforehand what we need to know, so that we can recognize the truth when we finally see it. Don't count on proof to persuade you to believe—it will probably let you down. Rather, believe now *before* you see, and, eventually, you may even understand.

PRAYER

Oh, my God, I am so dense! You teach me things repeatedly in Your word, yet because I can't fully wrap my brain around them, I make excuses and set them aside, neither believing nor disbelieving Your instructions. Help me, Master, to find the faith to trust and walk in everything You say, even if I don't have a clue how it's all going to actually work. I praise You, Yeshua, for You do not consider the confounding of my mind to be an obstacle to my faith. Show me, ADONAI, how to press through my ignorance, and realize that Your word is all the proof I need.

IF WE WALK IN THE LIGHT

> If we say, "We have sharing with Him," but walk
> in the darkness, we lie, and do not do the truth.
> But if we walk in the light, as He is in the light,
> we have sharing one with another, and the blood
> of יֵשׁוּעַ, Yeshua, His Son, cleanses us from every
> sin. If we say, "We have no sin," we lead ourselves
> astray, and the truth is not in us. *But* if we confess
> our sins, He is faithful and righteous that He
> will forgive us the sins and cleanse us from every
> unrighteousness. If we say, "We have not sinned,"
> we make Him a liar, and His word is not in us....
> He who is saying, "I have known Him," but is not
> paying attention to His command—he is a liar, and
> the truth is not in him. –יוֹחָנָן א 1 YOCHANAN 1:6-10, 2:4

Let's be honest: we're all a bunch of liars—or, at least, we very
well might be. Sometimes, what we say to convince ourselves
(and others) that we are right with God is designed only for
deception. Perhaps it's time to consider our confession and
confront ourselves with the truth. Only in this may we make
our joy full.

If we say, for example, "We have sharing with Him," but in
fact, we "walk in the darkness," then "we lie, and do not do
the truth"—we are nothing but hypocrites. We cannot walk
where God is not, yet claim that we are with Him. Such insincerity only breeds harm and fosters our festering delusion.
And if we also say, "We have no sin," then "we lead ourselves
astray." And in so doing, we "make [God] a liar," and nullify
the sacrifice of His Son. Indeed, from what have we been
cleansed if we say, "We have not sinned"? To make such a

claim is to expose an emptiness within us—that inside, we actually possess neither the truth nor His word. And "[he] who is saying, 'I have known Him,' but is not paying attention to [Yeshua's] command," proves precisely the opposite: that, in reality, "he is a liar, and the truth is not in him."

The Master's will is nothing less than what He tells us to do; it is exactly the substance of what He speaks. The word of God enables us to intersect with His character, yet He is only knowable if He has our obedience. Should we choose, therefore, to no longer be betrayers of reality, we must stop relying on false hope and pride. Where we are walking in the darkness, we must turn instead to His light; where we have convinced ourselves we are sinless, we must instead humble ourselves and confess; and where we believe we have known Him while faithfully following our own way, we must instead submit to His authority and give our full attention to His word.

ADONAI is faithful to "forgive us the sins and cleanse us from every unrighteousness." Walk, then, as Yeshua walked, confess your sins, and pay attention to His word. Be fully convinced of reality and truth, and keep lying to yourself no more.

PRAYER

Master Yeshua, please open my eyes; let me no longer hide from my guilt and shame. Help me to see my walk with You as it truly is, that I may stop pretending, and come boldly and humbly to You for Your loving-kindness and cleansing. Your word lies always before me, my God, shining the honest light of Your perfect commands. Let me share You, be close to You, and truly know You, Yeshua. Fill me with Your word and Your truth…

ASK ANYTHING

> And this is the boldness in speech that we have toward Him: that if we ask anything according to His will, He hears us, and if we have known that He hears us, whatever we ask, we have known that we have the requested *things* that we have requested of Him. –יוֹחָנָן א 1 YOCHANAN 5:14-15

When just one too many prayers seem to go unanswered, it's no wonder we are tempted to lose faith. We are repeatedly told by God's word that we have that for which we have asked, yet, all too often, we appear to be left empty-handed. How are we supposed to maintain our grasp on a belief that does not yield either answers or results? What is the use of trusting a God who does not appear to keep His word?

Our aim must never be set solely on our circumstances; rather, we must see our present situation as just one point along an enduring path that promises to lead to the eternal. Our hope for victory over this world is embedded in our faith that Yeshua is the Son of God. Our belief in His Name grants us the unshakable knowledge that as He is the Life, and we are in Him, we are already living that age-enduring existence.

This, then, should give us great boldness towards God to speak frankly to our needs. Whatever our struggles or obstacles may be, we can freely and confidently bring them before our God... but there is a catch. We may ask Him for absolutely anything, and know beyond a doubt we have been heard, but only if it is "according to His will." How, then, do we know where our desires end and His will begins? We must first seek His will before we can seek His face.

Whatever we ask, then, according to His will, "we have known that we have the requested *things* that we have requested of Him." When it doesn't look as if we "have" anything even close to what we have requested, we have to believe that we either asked not according to His will, or that His answer fulfills our request in a way we do not understand. Our flesh and mind may find this arrangement wholly unsatisfying, but, in our spirit, we must trust that whatever today's struggle may be, in Yeshua, it will be eternally resolved tomorrow.

Why wouldn't God want to heal you, or rescue you, or change your circumstances today? "Does clay say to its Framer, 'What are you making'" (Isaiah 45:9)? It is not for us to question and wonder why our prayers seem to go unanswered, but rather to seek His will so that we may know we have been heard, and to believe that we have received the requested thing—no matter what it looks like.

In every circumstance, let us glorify God with our actions and faith, fully believing that He knows what He's doing. Keep pursuing His will, keep seeking His face, and then trust Him with whatever you ask.

PRAYER

Master Yeshua, I am Your slave, and I trust You completely to take care of me. Your wisdom is perfect, Your judgment is good, and I gratefully rest in Your hands. Help me, Master, in my ignorance and grief; help me to not insist on understanding, but only to submit to Your will. I come before You, Father, in boldness and in faith. Please hear and honor my requests in the way only You can.

BUT I HAVE THIS AGAINST YOU

> "To the Messenger of the Called-Forth in Ephesus, write... 'I have known your actions and your labor and perseverance, and that you are not able to bear *with* evil ones, and that you have tested those saying themselves to be emissaries but are not, and have found them liars; and you have persevered and carried *on* because of My Name, and have not been weary. But I have *this* against you: that you left your first love! Remember, then, from where you have fallen, and reform, and do the actions *you did at* first.'" REVELATION 2:1-5A

In the end, when we are standing before the Master, our hope is that He will be pleased with us. What a shocking blow it would be, then, if He weren't.

In Yeshua's final revelation to the Called-Forth community in Ephesus, the Son of Man praised their good actions: They had been laboring for Messiah's cause and persevering in it—showing no tolerance whatsoever for those who were doing evil. They refused to accept the claims of self-styled emissaries, but tested them in their assertions and found them to be liars. And they earnestly carried on and did not grow weary in the work because of the glorious Name of Yeshua.

But can the same be said of us?

Do we labor tirelessly in the spreading of the Good News and persevere in the making of disciples? Or do we just consume feel-good, faith-based content, and traffic in political ideology and rage? Do we refuse to abide evil in our circles of influence? Or do we fail to confront the repeated compromise of

God's word in false beliefs and fleshly behavior? Do we test those who occupy positions of spiritual authority in our eyes? Or do we blindly accept whatever they say, never weighing their teachings against Scripture, nor seeking to discern any hidden motives or corrupt character?

If we have fallen short in these and other ways, then how much more have we fallen away and left our first love? How much more have we walked away from the author of our faith? How much more have we forgotten the One who truly loves us: Yeshua?

In the adultery of our hearts we are following a different Messiah whenever our actions neglect to reflect the love we profess for our Savior. Don't be satisfied with emotional passion, but be filled with the passion to act and to do what is right, that you may never ooze into complacency, nor be complicit with any unrighteousness.

Your first love awaits you; come back to Him now... today. Return, and He will only hold against you His eternal and loving embrace.

PRAYER

O Yeshua, my Master and my love, I praise You and glorify You; I magnify Your Name and live only to serve You. Be pleased with me, ADONAI, and find me blameless before You. Let me not labor in my own futility and work for my own pleasure. Awaken me, O God, to the memory of who I am in You, that I will not forget to walk in righteousness, nor have tolerance for any form of evil. Here I am, Yeshua! I am coming back to You. Remind me, Master, from where I have fallen, that I may return in both my heart and actions, and may truly—and forever—love You.

GLOSSARY OF HEBREW TERMS

This glossary is alphabetized according to transliterated English. For simplicity's sake, punctuation has been ignored as far as alphabetizing is concerned.

Each entry includes the Hebrew, followed by its transliteration (as found in the Scripture quotations), followed either by the anglicized form of the word in parentheses, or, when warranted, by English translation or definition.

Pronunciation Guide

The chart below lists the English transliteration of each Hebrew consonant. Most pronunciations sound like their transliterations, such as ב (beit) = "b". That said, ח (cheit) deserves special mention. Represented in the transliteration as "ch," ח is sounded not in the front of the mouth (as in "much" or "church"), but gutturally, in the back of the throat (as in "Bach" or "loch")—not a sound normally heard in the English language. Similarly, the sound for כ (khaf), represented by "kh," is virtually identical to the guttural ח.

HEBREW	TRANSLITERATION	HEBREW	TRANSLITERATION	HEBREW	TRANSLITERATION
ב	b	כ or ך	kh	ס or שׂ	s
ח	ch	ל	l	שׁ	sh
ד	d	מ or ם	m	ט or ת	t
פ	f	נ or ן	n	צ or ץ	tz
ג	g	פ	p	ב or ו	v
ה	h	ק	q*	י	y
כ	k	ר	r	ז	z

* pronounced like "k"

Additionally, vowels in Hebrew are represented primarily according to a vowel pointing system; that is, a series of dashes and dots in proximity to the letters. Vowel points may appear in relation to any letter of the alphabet. In the following chart, the א is used as an example, though the א (as also the ע) has no associated sound by itself. The vowels are therefore pronounced and represented in the transliteration as follows:

HEBREW	TRANSLITERATION	PRONUNCIATION
אַ or אָ	a	"ah"
אֶ or אֵ	e	"eh"
אִ	i	"ee"
אֹ or וֹ	o	"oh"
אֻ or וּ	u	"oo"
אַי or אָי	ai	"ah-ee"
אֶי or אֵי	ei	"eh-ee"
אִי	iy	"ee"
אְ	'	~ stop ~

A

Adonai

In small capital letters, this represents יהוה, known as the tetragrammaton, and commonly referred to as God's sacred name. In English, יהוה is often represented as YHVH, or YHWH. Many English bibles render it as "the Lord" in small capital letters, and sometimes, "Jehovah."

א, Alef

first letter of the Hebrew alphabet, "first"

אָמֵן, **amen** (amen)

עֲמֹרָה, **'Amorah** (Gomorrah)

אַבְרָהָם, **Av'raham** (Abraham)

B

בַּר־נַבָּא, **Bar-Naba** (Barnabas)

ב, **Beit**

second letter of the Hebrew alphabet, "second"

בֵּית־עַנְיָה, **Beit-An'yah**

Bethany

בְּרֵאשִׁית, **B'reshiyt**

in the beginning, "Genesis"

C

חַוָּה, **Chavah** (Eve)

E

אֵל שַׁדַּי, **El Shadai**

God Almighty

אֶלְעָזָר, **El'azar** (Lazarus)

אֵלִיָּהוּ, **Eliyahu** (Elijah)

אֱלֹהִים, **'Elohiym**

God

G

גַּבְרִיאֵל, **Gav'riyel** (Gabriel)

גֵּיהִנֹּם, **Geihinom**

"Gehenna"; that is, "hell"

גּוֹיִם, **Goyim**

people of non-Jewish ethnicity; people-groups; "Gentiles"

H

הַכֹּהֵן, **HaKohen**

the Priest

הַשָּׂטָן, **HaSatan**

the Adversary, "Satan"

I

עִמָּנוּאֵל, **Imanuel** (Immanuel)

עִבְרִים, **Iv'riym** (Hebrews)

K

כֵּיפָא, **Keifa** (Cephas/Peter)

כְּפַר-נַחוּם, **K'far-Nachum**

Capernaum

כֹּהֲנִים, **Ko'haniym**

Priests

כֹּהֵן, **kohen**

priest

כֹּהֵן גָּדוֹל, **Kohen Gadol**

High Priest

כֹּהֵן הַגָּדוֹל, **Kohen HaGadol**

the High Priest

M

מַרְתָּא, **Mar'ta** (Martha)

מַתִּתְיָהוּ, **Matit'yahu** (Matthew)

מִרְיָם, **Mir'yam** (Mary)

מֹשֶׁה, **Mosheh** (Moses)

N

נֹחַ, **Noach** (Noah)

O

אוֹי, **oy!** (woe!)

P

פְּרוּשִׁים, **P'rushiym**

Pharisees

פֶּסַח, **Pesach** (Passover)

Q

קְדוֹשִׁים, **Q'doshiym**

holy ones, "saints"

R

רַבִּי, **Rabiy** (Rabbi)

רוּחַ, **Ruach** or רוּחַ, **ruach**

Spirit or spirit

רוּחַ אֱלֹהִים, **Ruach 'Elohiym**

(the) Spirit of God

רוּחַ הַקֹּדֶשׁ, **Ruach HaQodesh**

the Holy Spirit

S

סְדֹם, **S'dom** (Sodom)

שָׁבֻעוֹת, **Shavuot**

(the Feast of) Weeks

שִׁמְעוֹן, **Shim'on** (Simon)

שֹׁמְרוֹן, **Shom'ron** (Samaria)

סִילָא, **Siyla** (Silas)

T

תּוֹמָא, **Toma** (Thomas)

תּוֹרָה, **Torah**

instruction, "Law," five books of Moses; exclusive of the Talmud or Rabbinic traditions of Judaism

צְדוּקִים, **Tzaduqiym**

Sadducees

Y

יַעֲקֹב, **Ya'aqov**

Jacob or "James"

יַרְדֵּן, **Yar'den** (Jordan)

יֵשׁוּעַ, **Yeshua**

salvation, anglicized as "Jesus"

יְהוּדִיָה, **Y'hudiyah**

Jewish, *female*

יְהוּדִים, **Y'hudiym** (Jews)

יִשְׂרָאֵל, **Yis'rael** (Israel)

יוֹחָנָן, **Yochanan** (John)

יְרוּשָׁלַיִם, **Y'rushalayim**

Jerusalem

Z

זְכַרְיָה, **Z'khar'yah**

Zacharias or Zechariah

זְקֵנִים, **z'qeniym** (elders)

ABOUT THE AUTHOR

KEVIN GEOFFREY, born Kevin Geoffrey Berger, is the first-born son of a first-generation American, non-religious, Jewish family. Ashamed of his lineage from childhood, he deliberately attempted to hide his identity as a Jew, legally changing his name as a young adult. After experiencing an apparently miraculous healing from an incurable disease, Kevin began to search for God. Eventually, he accepted Yeshua as Messiah, a decision which would ultimately lead him to be restored to his Jewish heritage. Today, Kevin is a strong advocate for the restoration of all Jewish believers in Yeshua to their distinct calling and identity as the faithful remnant of Israel.

Kevin has been licensed by the International Alliance of Messianic Congregations and Synagogues (IAMCS), and ordained by Jewish Voice Ministries International (JVMI) and the Messianic Jewish Movement International (MJMI). He has been involved in congregational planting, leadership development, and itinerant teaching, but is best known as a writer, having authored eight books to date, including the *Messianic Daily Devotional* and *Bearing the Standard: A Rallying Cry to Uphold the Scriptures*. Kevin is also the editor of the *Messianic Jewish Literal Translation of the New Covenant Scriptures (MJLT NCS)*. In addition to writing about uniquely Messianic Jewish topics, Kevin's clear and impassioned teachings focus on true discipleship, radical life-commitment to Yeshua, and upholding the Scriptures as God's perfect standard.

Kevin is a husband, a father, and also the principal laborer of both Perfect Word Ministries and MJMI. He currently resides in Phoenix, Arizona with his wife Esther and their four cherished sons, Isaac, Josiah, Hosea and Asher.

OTHER BOOKS BY
PERFECT WORD PUBLISHING

Messianic Daily Devotional

Messianic Mo'adiym Devotional

Messianic Torah Devotional

The Messianic Life:
Being a Disciple of Messiah

Deny Yourself: The Atoning
Command of Yom Kippur

Behold the Lamb (Passover Haggadah)

The Real Story of Chanukah

Bearing the Standard: A Rallying
Cry to Uphold the Scriptures

Messianic Jewish Literal Translation of the
New Covenant Scriptures (MJLT NCS)

resources.perfectword.org
1-888-321-PWMI

A ministry of Perfect Word Ministries

Lightning Source UK Ltd.
Milton Keynes UK
UKHW021831081222
413600UK00013B/315